The Disappearance of Ray Gricar

Pete Dove

Published by Trellis Publishing, 2021.

While every precaution has been taken in the preparation of this book, the publisher assumes no responsibility for errors or omissions, or for damages resulting from the use of the information contained herein.

THE DISAPPEARANCE OF RAY GRICAR

First edition. July 1, 2021.

ISBN: 979-8224098095

Written by Pete Dove.

THE DISAPPEARANCE OF RAY GRICAR

PETE DOVE

The Missing Attorney

Some problems become more troublesome the longer they are left. The aching molar which remains untended; the lawn which is left uncut. The same might be said of the case of Ray Gricar. Although, of course, the disappearance and possible death of a man, one with a high local profile, is much more serious than sore teeth or an unkempt yard.

Gricar was last seen on Friday April 15th 2005. It was a glorious day – one of the first of the year in which Spring had lightened the sky and warmed the air. Gricar had awoken at the normal time. He was living with his girlfriend, Patty Fornicola, in his comfortable Bellefonte, Pennsylvania home.

Bellefonte is just the sort of place you would expect a successful person such as a District Attorney to live. While it might sit someway to the north of the home of most of John Grisham's lawyer crime novels, in many other respects it would sit comfortably in the successful writer's repertoire. Victorian architecture proliferates, a reminder of its long past. It even features a town square on which the courthouse stands. The town was born back as far as 1794: a house, a crossroads and a mill, which was about to change hands. Then iron was discovered and the population grew, although today it still numbers under seven thousand inhabitants.

The town is wealthy, white, and working, with one of the lowest unemployment rates in the country. We can all get the picture. It is easy to see why its county's DA made it his home.

However, whether Ray's decision to take the day off work that morning was a spontaneous one or had been brewing in his mind for a while is something we do not know. Certainly, Patty Fornicola had not expected her boyfriend to decide to take his quirky red Mini Cooper down to Lewisburg, a little over an hour's drive away, that day. It may well be that she was surprised to take his call, later in the morning,

telling her he had skipped work, and was in the city. But equally, Gricar was senior enough to dictate his own hours, and the decision to do something different was not overly unusual, despite his commitment to his work.

His absence initially caused little stir. Patty reported him missing at 11.30pm on the night he disappeared, assuming that he had been involved in a car accident. Missing adults, especially mature men, do not bring instant attention from the police, even when that person is a prominent, elected official. Nor do they garner huge interest in the media. Two days after Gricar was last seen, the local newspaper reported the story on its front page but tucked it away in a bottom corner.

'Centre County DA Missing' read the headline of the small story printed in the Susquehanna Valley Daily newspaper.

'Police searched the land and air in central Pennsylvania for any sign of a car driven by Centre County's top prosecutor, who was reported missing Saturday after he failed to return home from a drive the day before,' continued the short account.

It seems as though Gricar made the journey, enjoying the early season warmth, and arrived in Lewisburg without issue. He parked on a lot close to the Street of Shops – the car was discovered there on the Saturday, the next day, by a local state trooper. The name, 'Street of Shops', is a little misleading; rather than a High Street or Downtown Mall, it is a large, indoor market, full of arts and craft type stalls. The perfect place to pick up an unusual artefact, or a gift for a loved one. Behind it flows the expanse of water that is the Susquehanna River. It appears that Gricar had left the car, and had made his way to nearby Market Street, one of the main thoroughfares through Lewisburg. Whether he actually spent time in the Street of Shops arcade is less clear, but a number of witnesses reported either speaking to Gricar or seeing him walking down Market Street on that morning.

The contents of his car were interesting. His phone, turned off, was discovered there. While many of us seem as though we are surgically attached to our cell phones these days, that was less the case back in 2005; further, a prosecutor deciding to take a day off of work might want to leave his phone behind, having made the decision not to turn it on for fear of being pestered with job related questions.

Absent from the car were Gricar's keys – which seems in line with expectation – and his wallet. Again, that is not strange. But also missing was his laptop, circa 2005. This would not be a slimline, lightweight tablet, but a hefty tool, and the sort of item that would only be carried if it was going to be used. The conclusion to draw is that the trip to Lewisburg was not just about pleasure. Of course, it is possible that the content on a state prosecutor's laptop might be sufficiently sensitive that he could not to take the chance of it falling into the wrong hands, but if it was genuinely too valuable to risk being stolen from his car, why would he bring the device with him in the first place?

If his disappearance was filled with mystery, Ray Gricar's early life was both plain and privileged. He was born in October 1945. He grew up in Cleveland, Ohio, being raised in the popular and comfortable Collinwood area of the city, bordering Lake Eyrie. He was sent to the highly regarded Gilmour Academy Catholic School, and from there to the nearby University of Dayton, a Marist organisation. His interest in law stemmed from these days, and followed a spell working as an intern in the Prosecutor's office there.

His passion spiked, he majored at Case Western Reserve University of Law back in Cleveland. Having qualified as an attorney, he became a prosecutor in Cuyahoga County, where he specialised in violent crime, especially murder and rape.

Shortly after taking a new direction in his career at State College, Pennsylvania in 1980, he took the decision to become a home father to his adopted daughter, Lara, while his wife worked at the State University. However, he was soon offered a post as an assistant at the

Centre County District Attorney's office, which he accepted. When the senior incumbent chose not to run in 1985, and with no other candidates putting their names forward, Gricar stood for the vacant post and won, unopposed. Back then, the role was a part time one, but Gricar successfully pressed for it to become a full-time position, and he was re-elected in 1989, 1993, 1997 and 2001. However, even had he not disappeared he would not have been re-elected in 2005. Now 59, he had announced that he was going to retire in December of that year, at the age of 60.

Gricar had married twice before setting up home with Patty Fornicola. The first wife, Barbara, he married in 1969 and divorced in 1991. His second marriage was much shorter – just five years from 1996 to 2001. He had been living with Patty for a little under three years when he disappeared.

During his time in office, he had once more specialised in prosecuting cases of homicide. Among the more notorious was the Hetzel Union Building shooting in 1996. Here a teenager, 19-year-old Jillian Roberts, armed herself with a 7 mm Mauser rifle, hid herself in some bushes and opened fire on fellow students at the Pennsylvania State University. Two students were wounded, one fatally.

Perhaps the most notorious case with which Gricar was associated was one he chose not to prosecute. That of football coach Jerry Sandusky. Sandusky had spent much of his career as assistant coach at the Pennsylvania State university. During his time there he set up 'The Second Mile', a not-for-profit charity which looked to support underprivileged youth, often focussing on those without a father figure at home, and who were in 'at-risk' groups. However, Sandusky was a pedophile, and used the charity as a front to groom young, pre-pubescent boys. He would shower them with gifts and treats and win their trust. Then, after sporting activity, the showering would continue, this time naked and with the boys. From there, he went on to sexually abuse some of them. In 2012 he was convicted of 45 counts of various types of abuse. Most of his victims were between the ages of 10 and 14.

However, thirteen years before, in 1998, complaints had been raised against Sandusky. Specifically, it is claimed, the mother of an alleged victim contacted the DA's office to report the allegation. As District Attorney at that time, Gricar declined to press charges. After Sandusky was convicted, there were rumours that Gricar had turned down the chance to prosecute not because of weaknesses in the case against the coach, but because the man had achieved legendary status in the State. However, an assistant to Gricar, who served with the DA for five years, disagreed. 'No one got a bye with Ray,' he said. 'He didn't care who you were; he had a job to do.'

A job which saw Ray Gricar grounded in the kind of career that could make him a target for revenge crimes.

Three days after Gricar was confirmed as missing, his daughter Lara issued a plea to her father. The tone suggested that, at that stage at least, she believed that he had chosen to hide himself away.

'I want more than anything to hear your voice and for you to hug me,' she told the microphones and cameras at the carefully convened press conference. 'Maybe we can go for a hike – go hike up a mountain and sit and talk. Please call.' The understandably emotional young lady widened her address to the public at large: 'To everyone else out there,' she continued, 'if you have seen my father, please contact police.'

However, the appeal brought no breakthrough, no return of Ray Gricar. Within a week, the FBI were called in. A missing DA is cause for concern. This led to divers searching the Susquehanna River, while helicopters scoured the land.

The underwater search delivered no results. But the river did later offer up some clues. Gricar's laptop was discovered three months after he went missing. It had, apparently, been dumped over the PA-45 bridge which sits over the river between Lewisburg and Milton, some five miles away. So, it is certainly possible that Gricar walked that relatively short distance. Equally, he could have travelled in another person's car. Or, the laptop could have been disposed of by a third party.

There was one particularly interesting factor in the discovery of the laptop. The machine's hard drive was missing. That was not something that could happen by accident. Could this be the reason Gricar had removed the laptop from the car? To dispose of it, with the hard drive somewhere else. Was there incriminating material on that machine?

It is impossible to say for sure, but one further clue points to the possibility that Gricar had some secret he wanted to stay buried. After his disappearance, police searched his home computer. The desktop revealed some interesting searches. 'How to wreck a hard drive', 'how to fry a hard drive', and 'water damage to a notebook computer' all appeared deep in the computer's search history. Removing a hard drive from a computer is not an easy job. Separating it from the machine, smashing it, and then throwing it in a river away from its home are among the most effective way of ensuring that it is never examined.

Several months passed before a fisherman fishing off the adjacent old railway bridge took a surprising catch. The missing hard drive. It was too damaged to be read.

Gricar was declared legally dead on July 25th, 2011. However, in this case, the declaration was more of a tidying up exercise than a statement of near certainty. The police in Pennsylvania still believe that leads might appear – they consider the case open and active.

'These types of cases are unique,' said Chief Miller of the Sunbury Police in January 2017. 'You have to think outside of the box. You have to make noise and let the dust settle. It is then when you can possibly get answers. With a click of a button, the media can reach thousands and go places we as police can't go. I wish all the investigators luck in solving the case of Ray Gricar.'

Theories abound as to what happened to the attorney. One of the stronger suppositions is that the serving DA was murdered by a former member of the Hell's Angels. The unnamed source behind this allegation, who claimed to be a former high-ranking member of the order, said that Gricar was killed in a revenge attack for a prosecution which resulted in a long prison sentence in the 1990s.

The source also claimed that the killer acted as an FBI informant, revealing to the Government agency details of criminal activities the organisation was planning, or had carried out. The revelations were made back in 2013 but have not resulted in the discovery of Gricar's body. Both the FBI and Pennsylvania police have interviewed the informant, who claims he came forward to ensure he did not face prosecution himself.

The former Biker gang member went as far as to take officers to the broad location of where the victim's body is buried, but he stopped short of revealing the actual site since he wanted guaranteed immunity from prosecution in return. As this was not forthcoming, the informant refused to reveal the precise location of Gricar's body. However, he did claim that the then DA had been tortured before he was killed.

Gricar's family took the claims that his body was buried with a healthy dose of cynicism, having been witness to previous assertions which proved false. His nephew, Tony Gricar, said:

'We've heard pretty much all the theories that anyone's ever come up with.'

A further well held theory related to the abuse scandal surrounding Sandusky. Speculation here has circulated that Gricar was murdered for not pursuing Sandusky when he had the chance, possibly resulting in many more assaults being committed. Theories have abounded that the possible killer could have been a victim, or one of their family members. Others that right-wing extremist groups saw the act of not pursuing prosecution as a betrayal of their view of society, one in which criminals such as Sandusky are soundly and severely punished for their crimes. While few would find it hard to argue in the defence of such criminals, most still recognise that the process of justice must be done and be seen to be done. Although many amateur, and presumably, a few professional detectives have tried for years to link the non-prosecution of Sandusky with Gricar's disappearance, they have been completely unsuccessful in doing so. Sandusky, for what it is worth, continues to claim his innocence of all charges, stating that while he enjoyed the company of children, it was for their honesty and openness, not for perverted reasons. He believes that the complainants were manipulated into alleging their charges against him.

Another theory was that Gricar, willingly or inadvertently, picked up a passenger in the car. This theory evolved from the forensic search of his Mini Cooper. Gricar was known to loath the smell of cigarette smoke and of smoking in general. He was a committed non-smoker. However, traces of cigarette ash were located on a mat in the footwell of the passenger side of the small car. Investigators also detected a noticeable cigarette smell. However, the theory that Gricar may have been forced into taking a passenger was weakened by the fact that there were no signs at all of foul play, or a fight, in the car.

The idea that Gricar is dead, the victim of violence, is the one which holds greatest support among the amateur sleuthing community. However, that is hardly surprising given the absolute lack of evidence pointing either that way, or any other way. The story is that much more dramatic if it ends with a body.

The notion that a prosecutor might just manage to make some enemies in his life is surely one which would have appeared to the police and FBI. Yet at no stage has any person who appeared in court to face Gricar's questions been listed as even as suspect. Nor have their family members. That is most probably because no such person contributed to his disappearance and likely death. However, of course the possibilities remain that either the authorities are yet to find any such evidence, or are in possession of it, but have kept this secret in order not to damage their ongoing enquiries. Nevertheless, both theories seem unlikely.

Inevitably, in some minds, thoughts turn closer to home. Had, in fact, those internet searches been carried out not by Ray himself, but by Patty? He had been through two divorces, so was the driven DA actually impossible to live with, and had he been so difficult that it had pushed his girlfriend over the edge? Did a large spaceship touch down from a distant planet, disgorge an army of Plutonian Pig-Aliens and carry Ray Gricar away for experiments? The last option seems just about as likely as the concept that Patty Fornicola killed her boyfriend. As is normal in such cases as this, police searched the family home and investigated close family. They, in turn, consented to polygraph tests. On this occasion the idea that this was to rule them out of suspicion proved correct; no person of interest emerged and neither Patty nor any other members of Ray's family are now, or have ever been, under suspicion. Those that suggest otherwise are merely speculating, and also causing further hardship to a family that has suffered enough.

Which leads us on to another theory regarding Ray's disappearance, that he had suffered so much that he killed himself.

It does have to be noted that Ray was not the only member of his family to disappear in strange circumstances. His brother, Roy, disappeared from his home in West Chester, Ohio, in May 1996. His body was discovered in the Great Miami River a week later. His death was ruled a suicide. Roy suffered from serious bouts of depression, and this mental illness can have its roots in genetics and be seen across families. Certainly, some friends and acquaintances did comment that the attorney had not seemed to be himself in the days and weeks leading up to his disappearance. But, then again, he had not appeared sufficiently different for most to note the fact other than in retrospect, when everybody's view becomes just that little bit less foggy, lit as it is by the not always honest light of tragedy.

The damaged computer hard drive lingers like a vaguely aching tooth, constantly nagging. We do not know that it was Ray who removed the drive, but it seems unlikely that a casual attacker would do so. If it was the victim himself who took the machine apart, could that have been a forerunner to killing himself? A way of ensuring that his reputation remained intact, and that his family could be saved from the media digging deep in his every action? Of course, such an outcome is possible, but just as with every other scenario created, one important factor is significantly lacking. Evidence. Without that, the theory is full of holes. Despite the best efforts of its supporters to keep it afloat, it sinks under the weight of its own inadequacies.

The concept that Ray Gricar simply decided to walk away from his old life is similarly fraught with problems. It has its supporters, but any link it has with reality is tenuous. Advocates of the new life theory take together the following random pieces of evidence. Firstly, that by destroying his computer he was ending his own link with his work; that he did have a track record of starting new relationships, that he was close to retirement, and wanted to make a fresh start.

Their theory is enhanced by the evidence of two shop owners in Lewisburg. One reported that they believed the six-foot-tall, heavily built attorney was waiting for someone in his shop. His distinguished grey, slightly receding hairline was memorable. The other that they saw him with a dark-haired woman. Was she a smoker? Was it her cigarette ash in the red Mini Cooper?

But then reality steps in. There was little or no evidence to suggest that Ray and Patty's relationship was struggling. Friends and colleagues stressed that Ray was hugely committed to both his family and his work. He loved his daughter intensely, and the concept that he would completely abandon her simply holds no logic.

Since his disappearance, Ray Gricar's cell phone, his bank account, his credit has never been used. Finally, and perhaps most significantly, the shopkeeper who saw the tallish man talking to the dark-haired woman was far from certain that the man was indeed Ray Gricar. Without this shopkeeper's testimony, the entire 'walk away' theory falls apart.

The authorities remain as much in the dark as everybody else. Shawn Weaver, as Bellefonte Police Chief, was in overall charge of the case for eight years, while it remained the responsibility of his department before it was handed it on to the Pennsylvania State Police Department. 'You can be set on one theory, really firmly believe it and they you can talk yourself right out of it,' he noted.

Stacy Miller Parks was also the District Attorney of Centre County for a while and later moved into media analytics. During her time in post not one clue emerged that might throw light on the disappearance of her predecessor. 'I'm not sure if we're ever really going to know what happened to him,' she said. 'Maybe someday, someone will give us that tip we need to close this book. I'm not entirely confident that's going to happen. I'm afraid this might just always be an unsolved case.'

Other even more ridiculous ideas have been purported from time to time – from the journalist sitting down with two men in a distant café, being told that he had better be aware he was getting into something dark and dangerous, to the notion that Gricar had somehow decided to run unscrupulous election campaigns. Given that he had already announced his retirement, that seems particularly unlikely.

Another idea suggests he ran away because he was facing a DUI charge; something surely that would have emerged from official channels if it bore even the slightest link to reality. The fact is, nobody knows what happened to him that warm Spring day in 2005. Whether he is alive or, sadly more likely, dead. Whether he took his own life or had it taken from him. The possible incident with Jerry Sandusky's case apart, Gricar's long reign as DA was remarkably uncontroversial. And we should not forget that the evidence presented to him about Sandusky was, at the time, extremely light. His failure to act sparked no huge outcry then, it was only after the coach's conviction that two and two were added together, and some found the answer to be 'conspiracy'. Ray Gricar was seen as hardworking and earned the respect of adversaries and friends in the courts of Centre County. He was not a political animal, seeking big cases and wide exposure. Just an ordinary guy doing an important job. Competently. No more, no less.

On nine separate occasions Ray's DNA has been compared to current lists of unidentified bodies and no hint of a match has ever been found. This supports the possibility that he is alive today. Todd Matthews worked for the National Missing and Unidentified Person System, known as Namus. He holds out hope for an outcome, one way or another, in this case. 'When a District Attorney goes missing, you, know, it's pretty big,' he said. It's going to catch people's attention. A lot of people don't have a large footprint. This guy had influential friends. He was well known.'

Although, at the same time, the USA is a big place; Pennsylvania is a big place. There are plenty of locations where a body could linger undiscovered forever. Including, of course, The Susquehanna River. Yet there have been many, unproven, sightings of Ray Gricar over the years. Especially in the early days after his disappearance. One report even claimed he was in the audience of the Oprah Winfrey Show, which was being recorded in Chicago. None of these, though, has ever stood up to scrutiny. People mean well, but sometimes in their enthusiasm to help the police with their enquiries, they can raise false hopes.

For the peace of mind of Patty, of Lara and of all his friends and colleagues, let us hope that Todd Matthews is right, and that one day a conclusion to this mysterious story is found. Until and unless that happens, the disappearance of Ray Gricar will continue to nag and pull at the lives of those who knew him. A toothache that won't go away.

THE ICE KILLER AND OTHER STORIES

RAY DUNCAN

Robert Hansen was dubbed the "Butcher Baker" by the media after he kidnapped, raped and killed at least seventeen women with possibly more victims that have yet to be identified. The murders took place in and around his hometown of Anchorage, Alaska as Hansen would hunt down his victims in the woods with a variety of weapons. It would take over twelve years before authorities would finally capture and convict Hansen in 1983. His case would remain out of the limelight until a movie called "Frozen Ground" would be released, detailing his exploits with John Cusack starring as Hansen.

EARLY YEARS

Hansen was born to Danish immigrants in Estherville, Iowa in 1939. Both of his parents were strict and Robert would be crippled by shyness for his entire life. He had a stutter and a bad case of acne which left pockmarks on both of his cheeks. His father, Christian, was a baker and Robert would eventually follow him into the same occupation. But his father was not a positive influence on him, routinely belittling his son. Robert had no escape, he was bullied both at home and at school.

At school, he was the proverbial social outcast. He would walk down the halls with his eyes downcast and very few people even noticed him. He only had a small handful of male friends who kept him at arm's length and virtually no female friends.

He had no success whatsoever with the opposite sex, being alternately ignored and ridiculed. This rejection would evolve into a seething hatred of all attractive women as his sexual fantasies about them turned into violent ones.

With no outlet, he took up hunting and found solace in the woods, shooting at animals.

At the age of eighteen, Robert would join the United States Army Reserve and would serve for one year before being discharged. The army service would give him a bit of self-confidence as Robert now attempted to talk to women and ask for dates. But women were taken aback by his awkward nature, his stutter and his thousand-mile stare behind black-rimmed glasses.

With his military experience, he would find employment at a police academy in Pocahontas, Iowa as an assistant drill instructor. Once there, he began badgering a secretary for a date until she filed a complaint against him. He would eventually meet his first wife in Pocahontas, marrying her in the summer of 1960.

The marriage would not last. Only a few months later, Robert would be arrested for burning down a school bus garage.

The bullying and torment Hansen experienced during his high school years would prove to be too much. He had to somehow, someway get back at his tormentors. So even three years after he graduated he decided to go back to his old school and burn down the garage that housed the school bus.

He would be sentenced to three years in jail during which his wife would file for divorce. He would serve a little over twenty months before being released.

The arson episode would prove to be another step on the ladder to Hansen's eventual homicidal psychosis. He was showing all of the earmarks of a serial killer; arson and cruelty to animals. He had felt powerless his whole life but would act out in fantasies where he would have power...whether it was by starting a fire or shooting a deer. Eventually, this need for power would lead him to a deep-seated desire to have power over the women who rejected him throughout his life.

ESCALATING BEHAVIOR

Robert would test the waters of criminal behavior starting with petty thefts. He would be arrested several times for theft, looking to be growing into a small time criminal until 1963 when he married his second wife.

Four years into their marriage, the couple would have two children and move to Anchorage, Alaska.

Robert would start work in a local bakery. Under his father's tutelage, he was a capable baker and hiring him was a no-brainer. But his co-workers found him to be a social misfit. He would brag to them about the strangest things, like his kleptomania and ability to steal things without getting caught.

JUST ANOTHER FACE IN THE CROWD

Hansen went out of his way to give off the appearance of a respectable citizen.

His neighbors liked him and he would set several hunting records in the area, decorating his home with the heads of big game and fish. He would open his own bakery in a downtown mini-mall, becoming friends with the regular customers and even servicing the policemen who came in for their morning donut.

No one, not his wife, children or his neighbors knew of the monster that lurked inside him.

But he couldn't keep the monster hidden long. In fact, the respectable front was just camouflage.

In 1967, Hansen would assault a young receptionist at gunpoint. He would plead no contest to the assault charge but serve very little time. A few months later, he followed a pretty eighteen-year-old girl home and again tried to sexually assault her.

He would serve very little time in jail, being sent instead to a psychiatric facility where he described his bizarre and dark sexual fantasies. He would tell his psychiatrist that he suffered from memory lapses and remembered little of what took place during his assaults.

The courts were lenient on Hansen to a fault.

In 1971, Hansen would kidnap and rape a seventeen-year-old waitress outside a coffee shop.

He would let her go but not without a threat.

"I will hunt you down," he hissed in her ear. "Hunt you down and kill you. I'm a respectable man. I own a business. You're just a kid. No one will believe you."

The teenage girl, scared out of her wits, believed him.

With no punishment or capture in sight, Hansen would become even bolder as he plotted out his mouth violent fantasies.

FIRST BLOOD

In what would seem to be a recurring theme for Hansen's victims, there was very little media coverage or follow-up investigations.

In 1973, a seventeen-year-old schoolgirl named Megan Emerick walked out of a dorm laundry room in Seward, Alaska and disappeared without a trace.

She is presumed to have been another of Hansen's victims though he would later deny it.

Unfortunately, Megan's disappearance would garner little in the way of press or law enforcement investigation. There were a few fliers and short articles in the local newspaper but little else offered.

Megan was a quiet girl who grew up in the peaceful town of Delta Junction. She liked to go out on the Yukon River to hunt and fish. A typical teenager, she liked rock music and horses but she left home at an early age to go to the Seward Skill Center, a place in Alaska where she would learn a vocation.

But on July 7th, she would disappear.

Years later, the vanishing teenage girls would be part of a growing trend in the Eklutna and Knik River areas.

LOST IN THE FOG

As construction of an eight-hundred-mile oil pipeline began in Alaska, a different population began filing into Anchorage. The oil money brought in prostitutes, pimps, and drug dealers who sought to service the oil workers who now had money to burn. The community began a transient one and sudden disappearances became nothing out of the ordinary. Anchorage became a frontier town, a city full of strangers where people disappeared without a trace.

Robert would initially target any woman who caught his eye. But he began to learn that strippers and prostitutes were less likely to have people come looking for them. He would soon develop his own modus operandi, a system that he would adhere to with religious fervor.

He would target solitary women under the guise that he was a photographer, offering compensation if they posed for him. Hansen would then arrange a meeting place in a coffee shop and wait outside, making sure that the woman arrived alone. Once assured that there would be no witness, he would arrive at the coffee shop and convince the woman to come leave with him for the photo shoot. They would get into the car and he would already have one-half of the handcuff attached to the passenger side drive handle. Once he got into the driver side, he would lean over and in one motion handcuff their wrist and take out the gun from his glove compartment.

Sometimes he would drive the women home or to an isolated motel room where he would rape them. Other times he would fly to a desolate area along the Knik River.

A STRANGE CODE

Robert didn't kill all of his victims. Sometimes he would rape them and release the ones who he thought really found him attractive. His reasoning was, they played out to his fantasy and didn't deserve to die.

Others, the ones who resisted and fought, he would pretend to set free. Then he would hunt them down through the woods and shoot them with his rifle.

By the summer of 1980, bodies of dead prostitutes began to be found in and around the Anchorage area. But finding dead bodies in the Alaska wilderness was not an out of the ordinary type thing. Hikers would often get lost in the wilderness and not know how to make their way back, succumbing to the elements.

The first would be a young woman believed to be in her late teens or early twenties. Workers in a building found a shallow grave on Eklutna Lake Road. The body was badly decomposed and half-eaten by bears. Police were able to make a facial reconstruction from the skull and published their approximation of the young woman's appearance to the local news outlets. The victim was never identified, however, and to this day is still known as "Eklutna Annie."

When her body was recovered, she was estimated to be in her late teens or early twenties. She was between 4'11" and 5'3" inches tall with long, reddish-brown hair. Hansen would admit that she was the first victim that he killed but that he didn't know her name.

Hansen said that she or her family lived in Kodiak. Investigators believed that she may have come from Washington or California.

What is certain is that she was a topless dancer or a prostitute that Hansen picked up, offering to pay for her services. He told her that he lived in Muldoon but when Hansen drove past the town the woman panicked. She tried to escape out of his truck but Hansen pulled a gun on her.

"Now look," Hansen said. "If you do exactly what I tell you and don't give me any problem whatsoever, there's going to be none, you won't get hurt in any way, shape or form."

"Eklutna Annie" could only nod in agreement out of fear. They continued to drive, her heart racing with fear, her mind racing with strategies on how she could escape.

But then Hansen's truck got lodged in the wet Alaska mud. Hansen allowed the young woman to step out of the vehicle to help put the truck back on solid ground.

Then she ran.

Hansen stated that he caught her by the hair as she took a knife out from her purse.

Overpowering the young girl, Hansen wrenched the knife away and stabbed her in the back.

Her body would be found on July 21st, 1980 buried near a power line.

MORE BODIES...

Joanne Messina was another body found near Eklutna Lake Road, buried in a gravel pit. Her body was badly decomposed and there was little evidence remaining. She worked as a topless dancer as did other Hansen victims such as Sherry Morrow and Paula Goulding.

Sherry Morrow was a striking beauty, with feathered blonde hair and heart-shaped lips. She was an aspiring model who turned to topless dancing to make ends meet. Like he would do so many times, Hansen would meet her under the guise of a photo shoot.

Sherry would be among the first that Hansen would play the "hunting game" with. After raping and torturing her, he flew her to the woods where he sent her blindfolded and handcuffed, telling her to run.

His sadistic fantasies now coming to life, Hansen would hunt her down. He would follow her through the woods as she cried and begged for her life.

He shot her in the back, rolled her over and ripped off a necklace from her neck.

A 'good luck' arrowhead locket that her boyfriend had given her.

It was the next step in his mind, to begin taking mementos and trophies of his victims. He would set them aside in a box then when he felt the need to relive the moment he could take the souvenir out, fingering it through his hands and relive the fantasies in his mind.

UPPING THE ANTE...

The adrenaline high that Hansen got when he first began killing started to subside. So he began the 'hunting game' in order to feed the monster inside. He had gone from petty theft to attempted sexual assault before graduating to rape and murder.

Now it was turning the rape and murder into a sport.

Sherry's body would be found on the banks of the Knik River. Sherry had been reported missing for over a year and her body was found in a shallow grave on the banks of the river. Two off-duty police officers were in the wilderness hunting moose when they came upon her decomposed remains. She had been shot in the back three times with what investigators believed to have been a hunting rifle. Her body was fully clothed but there were no bullet holes in her clothing. Investigators believe that she had been naked when Hansen shot her after which he put her clothes back on.

Police were able to identify Sherry's body from dental records. She had been reported missing over a year ago by her boyfriend. The clothes they had found on her skeletal remains were the same as the clothes described by her boyfriend.

The case would go nowhere, however. The police told the boyfriend that the killer had over a year to cover his tracks. Finding him would be next to impossible.

Paula Goulding would meet the same fate as Sherry Morrow. Only seventeen-years-old and looking for work, the unemployed secretary started work as an exotic dancer to pay her rent. She would be targeted by Hansen and fall victim to him in the same way Sherry did. He would capture her, send her into the wilderness blindfolded where he would chase her down then after she couldn't run anymore, shoot her down like an animal.

Paula's body had been found in the exact same fashion, shot in the back but then redressed after death.

Sue Luna's body would be found two years later, the young Asian woman was forced to strip herself naked while Hansen made her run like a dog through the woods. The game was intoxicating to him as he shot her in the back after a lengthy chase.

Delynn Frey, Teresa Watson, Angela Feddern, Tamara Pederson, Lisa Futrell, and Andrea Altiery would all become victims of Hansen. He would collect "trophies" from each of them, taking a custom-made fish necklace from Andrea Altiery that would later be a critical piece of evidence when he would be captured.

But that capture when not come until June 13th, 1983 when Hansen encountered seventeen-year-old prostitute Cindy Paulson.

A STREET SMART STREETWALKER

Hansen was trolling for his next victim when he spotted Cindy selling her wares on an empty street. He had enticed Cindy to come into his car for $200 in exchange for oral sex. Cindy didn't feel threatened by the man, she got into his car without a second thought.

Hansen struck fast. He reached over and handcuffed her to the door then held a wood handled revolver to her head.

"Not a s-s-s-sound," the man stuttered as he put the car into drive. He drove her to his home in Muldoon. The alert Cindy began taking notes in her mind. The home was in a relatively well-to-do area. Once she entered, she found the home to be well kept and with nice furniture and full of hunting trophies. Hansen took her down to his den where there was a chain hanging from the ceiling. He tied her to the chain and stripped off her clothes. He would hold her captive for hours, alternating between raping and physically torturing her.

Hansen would grow tired and chained her by the neck to a post in the basement. Hansen then laid on the couch and went to sleep.

Upon awakening, Hansen untied Cindy and threw her in his car.

"If you t-t-t-try to get anyone's attention," Hansen hissed at his captive. "I will k-k-k-kill both you and them."

Hansen then bragged that he already had a rock solid alibi. He had convinced a friend to lie for him.

Hansen took his captive to the Merrill Field airport.

"We're flying out to my cabin," he snarled.

Cindy laid down on the back seat of the car, her hands cuffed in front of her body but her legs free. The car parked and she watched as Hansen began packing gear into his Piper Super Cub (a small two-seat airplane). Seeing her opportunity, Cindy scooted out of the back seat, opened the driver's side door and sprinted toward the nearest street.

Hansen turned around in time to see Cindy running but luckily for the young woman she made it to the busy street.

Robert Yount slammed on his brakes of his trucks on the rainy road. He opened up the passenger side door and picked up the young woman, immediately taken aback by her disheveled appearance. He drove her to the Mush Inn where Cindy ran inside, telling the clerk to call her boyfriend.

Yount would drive on to work where he called the police himself and told her about the half-naked, handcuffed woman he had dropped off at the Mush Inn.

Anchorage police officers arrived at the Inn but Cindy had disappeared. The clerk told them that she had taken a cab to the Big Timber Motel where her boyfriend stayed.

Police would go to the hotel and find her in room 110 of the motel. She was still handcuffed and alone. She told the police about Hansen, describing him as a wiry, scruffy man. He was tall at six feet but she thought he was non-threatening because he spoke with a stutter. She told of her hours of torture and rape, being hung up by her wrists and taken to the airport. The whole story sounded like something out of a horror movie but the detectives believed Cindy. She was street smart and scared out of her wits. The police drove her out to the hospital but then Cindy insisted on stopping by the airport.

Cindy was then able to positively identify the same plane that she saw Hansen toss weapons inside of. They also talked to a security guard who obtained the license plate of Hansen's vehicle. With a description and now an address in hand, detectives set out to Hansen's home.

Their suspect would arrive shortly after they staked out his home. Everything about him was exactly as Cindy described. He was wiry, nervous and spoke with a stutter.

As non-threatening as could be.

The inside of his home was also like Cindy as described. A moose head on the wall, trophies and news clippings of his hunting exploits.

A hidden panel in his wall would reveal a large cache of weapons.

All of this was legal, however. There was no evidence that Cindy had been raped. The only evidence was that she had been inside his home.

"I was at my friend's house," Hansen explained. "I was repairing a seat for my airplane then I went to the home of another friend. I left his house then went to the airport and installed the seat."

Hansen would deny Cindy's allegations during his interrogation. He deflected, stating that Cindy was telling them lies because he would not pay her extortion demands.

Hansen had an arrest record but his shy and quiet nature put some doubt in the mind of the cops. Police corroborated his alibi with his friend, John Henning, and the case went cold.

Cindy identified Hansen in a police lineup and insisted that he was the man who raped her. Things went south in the investigation, however, when Cindy refused to take a lie detector test. She had an inherent distrust of police and if they wouldn't take her at her word, she was willing to put the whole thing behind her.

She knew that Hansen was taking her on a one way trip to her death and she escaped. She also knew that the police didn't take prostitutes seriously.

So she walked.

She drifted in and out of the area and couldn't be reached when the police wanted to follow up. The case would be suspended.

But Detective Glenn Flothe of the Alaska State Troopers had already made the determination that the several bodies found around the area was the work of one man.

A serial killer.

And there was something about Robert Hansen that made alarm bells go off. He had a task force go out to the red light districts of Anchorage and warn the women that a serial killer was on the loose.

Then he got the FBI involved.

BRING IN THE BIG GUNS...

Flothe would team up with FBI special agent Roy Hazelwood in developing a psychological profile of the kind of man they were looking for.

Hazelwood believed that the killer was a man who was an experienced hunter but with low self-esteem. He would have a history of problems with women and would keep "souvenirs" of his kills such as a piece of jewelry or article of clothing. Hazelwood also believed that the killer would be socially awkward with a speech impediment.

Flothe used the profile and quickly narrowed down his investigation to Hansen. They would go to Hansen's home and bring him in for investigation. His team would then get a warrant to search Hansen's house, cars, and plane. They would discover jewelry belonging to the missing women as well as a cache of weapons hidden under the insulation in Hansen's attic. They would find the rifle they believed was used to kill two of the topless dancers as well as the revolver with the wooden handle he used to kidnap Cindy Paulson.

The mother lode, however, was an aviation map with little "x" marks all over it, indicating where Hansen had murdered his victims.

The search warrant was being executed at the same time that Hansen was placed into the interrogation room.

Investigators had decorated the room with pictures of his victims, maps of where they found the woman's bodies and crime scene photos.

They wanted to get inside his head, to let him know that they were on to him.

The man who psychologically tortured so many women was now having the script flipped on him.

INTERROGATION AND REVELATION

Another break in the case would come when the neighbor of Hansen noticed the police outside his home. She inquired as to what was going on and was told that Hansen was under investigation for murder. She quickly recanted her husband's story, stating that he had lied to cover up for Hansen and he did not know the extent of his crimes.

Investigators demanded an explanation of why Hansen had possession of the necklaces of the dead women. Hansen would deflect and deny until the interrogators finally cornered him. He would then get defensive, blaming the women and justifying his actions until he finally cracked.

"I started in 1971," Hansen said. "They were usually young. Like sixteen and nineteen. I didn't move to the prostitutes and strippers until later. I would get mad at them sometimes, sure. They would raise their prices on me."

Hansen would be arrested and charged with assault, kidnapping, multiple weapons possession as well as theft and insurance fraud (Hansen had filed a fake claim stating that someone had stolen his trophies. He used the proceeds to buy his private plane.)

Striking a plea bargain, Hansen would participate in telling the police about the markings on his aviation map in order to locate the bodies of his victims. He did this on the condition that they left his family alone and that it would not be publicized. An agreement was reached and Hansen would plead guilty to the murders of Morrow, Messina, Goulding and "Eklutna Annie".

"I began killing in the early 1970s," Hansen said. "Sometimes I would let the girl go. But only if she could convince me that she would not go to the cops."

Hansen would lead police to over seventeen grave sites. He would refuse to give up three marks on his map (two of these are suspected to belong to the spots where he killed Mary Thill and Megan Emrick, both of whom Hansen has denied killing.)

Hansen would be sentenced to 461 years plus life in prison without the possibility of parole. He would later be sent to the Anchorage Correctional Complex for health reasons and would die at the age of 75 on August 21st, 2014.

The identity of "Eklutna Annie" remains unknown.

STRANGLER JOHN

JOHN DENIS

John Reginald Christie was a prolific serial killer active in England during the 1940s and 1950s. He murdered at least six women including his wife—and some believe this number is higher, as well as a baby—before being arrested, convicted, and hanged. He lured women to his flat under the guise of assisting them with some medical procedure such as abortion and strangled and raped them; oftentimes while they were unconscious or dead, thus giving rise to allegations that he was a necrophiliac. Christie also likely framed his neighbor Timothy Evans for the death of Evans' wife and infant daughter for which Evans was convicted and hanged.

EARLY LIFE

John Reginald Halliday Christie was born in Halifax, Yorkshire, England on 8 April 1899. His father was a strict disciplinarian who was often abusive and mother and sisters were domineering. Yet, he was his mother's favorite so while Christie's father despised his frailty his mother emasculated him with over protection. His four older sisters also reinforced his mother's protective nature but they also dominated him. One incident when he was ten disturbed him profoundly; that of seeing one of his sister's legs up to the knee which made him physically attracted to her. This likely contributed to Christie's development into a controlling, sexually-dysfunctional hypochondriac with an intense hatred and fear of women because he simultaneously desired those who tempted him but, consequently, knew he could not satisfy them.

Christie's maternal grandfather died when he was eight and when asked if he wanted to see the body during the wake, Christie said yes. He felt pleasure and a release of the tension he always felt when the man was alive because his grandfather was rather frightening and these feelings fascinated him. He started playing in the graveyard and liked to look inside the cracks of the broken vault where children's coffins were kept.

In school, Christie did rather well and got along even though he did not cultivate any long-term meaningful friendships. At age 11 he won a scholarship to Halifax Secondary School where he proved rather adept at mathematics and algebra, and also with high-detailed work. He had an IQ of 128, was a scout, and sang in his church's choir; however, he grew increasingly unpopular with his classmates and was often ridiculed for his ineptitude with girls being given the names "Can't Make it Christie" and "Reggie no Dick." By puberty Christie had associated sex with dominance, violent aggression, and death which rendered him impotent unless he was in complete control. At this time he would also feign illness—becoming a hysterical hypochondriac—to get attention.

Christie left school at age 15 and became an assistant movie projectionist. When World War I began Christie enlisted as a signalman. He allegedly was rendered unconscious and temporarily blind by a mustard gas attack and lost his voice for three years; however, physicians attributed his blindness and muteness as a hysterical reaction instead of a true physical ailment. Thus, Christie's fear led to his hypochondria and he would exaggerate illnesses to avoid unpleasant situations. More simply, he was a coward.

After his stint in the army, Christie became a clerk. On 10 May 1920 Christie married 22-year-old Ethel Waddington from Sheffield. She was a plump, homely, passive, and sentimental woman who many believed was afraid of her husband even though he was mostly mute during this time. The couple looked down upon others and, subsequently, maintained a high degree of privacy but also seemed quiet and rather pleasant, devoted to each other, and to their dog and cat. His ongoing impotence with his wife led to his frequent visits to prostitutes—which began when he was 19—when she was out of town.

After they married Christie became a postman. He once stole some postal orders and was, consequently, sent to prison for three months. Following his first period of incarceration Christie regained his voice during a temper tantrum with his father only to lose it again for six more months before being able to speak again. When he was 25,

Christie was placed on probation with the post office after being charged with violence and accused of frequenting prostitutes. Christie subsequently left his wife and moved to London while she remained in Sheffield with her relatives.

Four years later, Christie was sentenced to prison for nine months on theft charges. Following this prison release he went through multiple jobs and lived with a prostitute who he physically assaulted with a cricket bat to the head and returned to prison for six more months. He was suspected of assaulting other women; however, the lack of evidence resulted in no arrests. A few years later he stole a car from a priest and was arrested again. After being released from prison this time he asked Ethel to move to London with him so they could be a married couple again.

Thus, in 1933 after a ten-year separation—and lonely at age 35—Ethel rejoined her husband, unaware of the type of man he really was or how her life would take a tragic turn.

Soon thereafter, Christie was hit by a car and required hospitalization which fueled his budding hypochondria. The literature suggests that over the course of 15 years Christie visited two physicians 173 times.

The Christies moved to the ground floor flat at three-story 10 Rillington Place in the Ladbroke Grove neighborhood of Notting Hill. At the time they moved here, Christie was a 40-year-old quiet inconspicuous man with reddish-ginger hair, light blue eyes, and an enormous forehead.

With World War II on the horizon, Christie signed up as a volunteer member of the War Reserve Police and became a Special Constable for Harrow Road Police Station for the next four years. Had his prior record been investigated—which it wasn't—there is no way that Christie would have received this appointment. Regardless, these four years were among Christie's happiest and he became almost fanatical about enforcing the law—so much so that he earned the nickname, "The Himmler of Rillington Place." Christie enjoyed wearing his uniform so much that the authority he had inflated his ego to the extent that he began to follow women and take notes of his endeavors. He also bored a peephole into his kitchen to watch his neighbors and ran down every single transgressor, no matter how minor the offense.

When his wife went to Sheffield to visit her relatives Christie developed a taste for peculiar sexual activities and found women who responded to his advances. One woman Christie met worked at the police station with him. She had a husband overseas in the war and Christie often spent time at her house with her. When her husband returned unexpectedly he filed for divorce and named Christie as a co-respondent after beating him up upon finding Christie in his house.

After this Christie began bringing women to his flat.

But first...

Timothy Evans

In the spring of 1948 Timothy and Beryl Evans moved into the third-floor flat. They were newlyweds and expecting their first baby. Timothy was 24 and Beryl was only 19; he drove a van for a living and was functionally illiterate. Known for his excessive drinking and often violent temper—likely due to his small stature of five-foot-five and 140 pounds—as well as his IQ of 70, propensity for lying, and proneness to self-aggrandizement, the Evans frequently quarreled. When the baby arrived—they named her Geraldine—Timothy's substandard income and Beryl's poor housekeeping and mothering skills caused them to fight even more, sometimes resulting in mutual physical violence. Beryl allegedly told Mrs. Christie that Tim had tried to strangle her and that she was pregnant again with an unwanted child. Beryl tried unsuccessfully to get rid of the baby.

It was around this time—the end of October 1948—that workers came to fix some floors and walls of 10 Rillington Place, as well as the community wash house.

In early November Beryl and Geraldine disappeared. There were conflicting accounts of their disappearance and subsequent murders; however, what is known is that that Christie offered to help Beryl with her pregnancy "problem" around noon one day. He is reported to have used rubber tubing to gas her for the procedure but she allegedly panicked so Christie began to hit her, and then strangle her, and then tried to have intercourse with her. When Evans came home that evening, Christie told him that the abortion hadn't worked and that if Evans went to the police it would only get them both in trouble and that police would not react well to reports that Evans and his wife fought often.

Christie proposed that he would dispose of Beryl's body and he hid her into the second-floor flat that belonged to Mr. Kitchener who was in the hospital at the time. Evans allegedly fed Geraldine and told Christie that he wanted to take his daughter to his mother's house but was dissuaded by Christie who told him that it would arouse too much suspicion. Christie told Evans that he knew a young couple who would take Geraldine and that Evans should tell people that Beryl and Geraldine were out of town on holiday.

Some speculate that Christie strangled the baby and put her with her mother in the second-floor flat and then blocked out what he had done.

Christie then told Evans to sell his furniture and leave town which Evans did.

Once the workmen were finished in the wash house Christie moved the bodies and hid them there. The following day he visited his doctor complaining of back pain. Despite Christie being a hypochondriac he had never had back problems. The doctor concluded that it was an injury sustained by unaccustomed exertion such as lifting a heavy weight.

Evans' mother Mrs. Probert did not buy her son's account that his wife and daughter were on holiday and discovered that her son staying with her sister, awaiting his wife. Mrs. Probert knew Evans was lying, that Beryl and Geraldine were missing, and that the furniture had been sold from their flat. After being confronted Evans stated that he disposed of his wife and put her body down the drain. He said that did not kill her and did not want to mention Christie because of the additional problems that would have caused. Evans said that he had met a man who gave him some medication to produce a spontaneous abortion but told Beryl not to use it. He said that when he returned from work he found her dead, took care of his daughter, and then pondered what to do next. Evans stated that he put his wife's body down the drain outside of the front door, stayed home from work, went in to give notice, and made arrangements for someone to take of Geraldine.

Police determined that Evans could not have disposed of Beryl the way he claimed to have done and he was arrested. During his interrogation and subsequent investigation Evans claimed that that he simply helped Christie put Beryl's body in the second-floor flat and that he had inquired of Christie about his daughter but was told that it was too soon to see her. Police searched the building and garden and in Evans' apartment near a pile of papers there were clippings from the newspaper about "a sensational torso murder, known as the Stanley Setty case" which was odd because Evans did not read, as well as a stolen briefcase.

During Evans' interrogation the Christies were also interviewed, she being coached by her husband.

Police went back to 10 Rillington Place and searched again. This time they found the decaying corpse of Beryl Evans, wrapped in a green tablecloth and tied with cord in the wash house, hidden behind some wood propped up against the sink. Underneath some wood behind the door was Geraldine's dead body with a man's tie still around her neck.

Dr. Donald Teare, the Home Office pathologist, performed the autopsy which showed that both had been dead about three weeks.

Beryl had bruises on her lip and right eye consistent with being hit and that she had been strangled with some type of a cord. There was no evidence that she had ingested anything to try to abort her three-month fetus but her vagina had bruising. The pathologist did not take a swab to check for semen.

Additional interrogations yielded different stories by Evans. He first admitted that he did, in fact, kill them both and that he was relieved to confess. He said he killed his wife because she was running up debts and then killed his daughter a few days later after he quit his job. On the days Evans said he hid the bodies, the carpenters were still working on the wash house so this could not be true. Further, his confession contained words that were beyond Evans' intellectual capacity and that if he had sold all of his furniture like he claimed then the baby's pram and highchair would not have been in Christie's flat—an indication that Evans expected to see his daughter again. The next confession was even longer and contradicted the first one. After Evans' mother came to see him following his arraignment he insisted that "Christie done it."

Evan's trial began on 11 January 1950 at the Old Bailey for the murder of his daughter although evidence of his wife's murder was included in the testimony. Prosecutor Christmas Humphreys wanted to avoid any testimony such that Beryl may have provoked Evans which could possibly warrant a reduced charge of manslaughter with a lesser sentence which is why he only pursued Geraldine's murder; because it was without motive and clearly cold-blooded. Christie was Humphreys' chief witness in the proceedings.

Evans' defense was in the hands of Malcolm Morris from Freeborough, Slack, and Company; however, there was little investigation done to assist Evans, likely to save on time and money. They also failed to question the carpenters and friend Joan Vincent, and neglected to look into Christie's criminal record; all of which may have provided the jury with reasonable doubt.

During the trial witnesses such as the carpenters and Mrs. Christie changed their testimony from their original statements to "fit" Evans' confessions with respect to dates and times. The furniture dealer wasn't contacted either which would have demonstrated that Evans was only following Christie's direction and that Christie had, in fact, lied. Compounding Evans' troubles was that Christie's composed persona on the stand impressed jurors due to he was articulate, reflective and presented himself as the victim. His demeanor was diametrically opposite Evans' "apparent dazed and guilt-ridden presentation." When Morris brought up Christie's criminal past the court was impressed with the fact that he had been on the straight-and-narrow for the past 17 years. Little did the court know what Christie had really been doing during that time.

It took the jury only 40 minutes to reach a guilty verdict Evans was sentenced to death and was hanged on 9 March 1950. He would later be granted a posthumous pardon after Christie's trial when the truth was revealed even though some still believe that Evans did murder his family.

The Crimes

Mrs. Christie wanted to move since the only other tenants in the flat were Jamaicans against whom she was highly prejudiced. Further, after Evans' trial Christie went into a deep depression and lost a lot of weight, and also lost his post office job due to courtroom testimony about his past crimes. Ever the hypochondriac, Christie checked himself into a psychiatric hospital for three weeks and continued to visit his doctor for stress-related symptoms; 33 times in eight months.

He found work as a clerk with the British Road Service and things seemed to improve; however, Christie soon gave notice, citing that he had found a better job which was not true. His wife was not pleased with him being unemployed and around the house all the time. On 11 December Mrs. Christie watched television with a friend, on the 12th she took laundry to Maxwell Laundries, and then was never seen again.

Nobody said she appeared to be distraught or that she said that she was going to take a trip.

Christie told her friends that she went to Sheffield and that he would follow shortly as he had a new job there. He told family members that his wife wasn't feeling well enough to write them.

At this same time Christie began to sprinkle his house and garden with disinfectant due to the increasingly putrid odor.

In January, Christie sold his furniture along with his wife's wedding band and watch. For more money he forged his wife's signature on a bank account she had and emptied it.

Shortly thereafter Christie met a Mrs. Reilly who was looking for a place to rent and he showed both her and her husband his flat. They paid him three months' rent in advance and kept his cat. Christie borrowed a suitcase, had his dog put down, and left. The Reillys ultimately left when the impending investigation commenced and they were told that Christie did not have the authority to sublet his flat.

Investigation

One of the upstairs tenants at 10 Rillington Place—Beresford Brown—noticed a hollow space behind a kitchen wall in Christie's old flat after the landlord gave him permission to use the kitchen since the flat was empty. Brown was looking for a place to mount a shelf for his radio and pulled away some of the wallpaper to try to open the door which he couldn't. When he shined a light through a crack he was horrified at what he found and called the police.

Chief Superintendent Peter Beveridge was on scene, as was Chief Inspector Percy Law of Scotland Yard, other officers, and the coroner. When the door was opened in the kitchen alcove they found a woman's corpse sitting in some rubble. Her back was to them and she was leaning forward. Behind her was something large wrapped in a blanket that was knotted to the victim's bra. Said bra was pulled up around her neck along with her black sweater and white jacket. Other than that she was nude save for a garter belt and stockings. She was taken from the cupboard and photographed and examined in the front room. She had been strangled with a ligature and her wrists were tied in front of her with a handkerchief tied into a reef knot.

Authorities focused on a second large object behind the woman and discovered it was another corpse. It had been propped on its head up against the wall. The blanket had been fastened with a sock tied in a reef knot around the ankles and the head was wrapped in a pillowcase that was also fastened by a stocking in a reef knot.

They noticed a third object. It was another body, also upside down, with her head beneath the second body. This one's ankles were tied with an electrical cord fashioned into a reef knot while a cloth covering her head was similarly knotted.

Investigators also took note of some loose floorboards in the rubble and found the wrapped body of Mrs. Christie amidst the rubble.

The first victim was a 20-something brunette who had been deceased for approximately one month. She had died from carbon monoxide poisoning and strangulation with a smooth type of cord. She had been sexually assaulted either at the time of her death or shortly thereafter. Scratches on her back indicated that she had been dragged across the floor. She was later identified as Hectorina McLennan, a 26-year-old prostitute.

The second victim was also a brunette and around 25 years of age. She, too, exhibited symptoms of carbon monoxide poisoning; particularly her pinkish skin color. She was also strangled and had had sexual intercourse around the time of her death. There was also evidence that she had been drinking heavily the day she died. She had poorly manicured hands and feet and was clad in a cotton cardigan and vest while another vest was fashioned into a diaper between her legs. It was estimated that she had died eight to 12 weeks earlier. She was later identified as 26-year-old Kathleen Maloney, also a prostitute.

The third victim was a mid-20s blonde, also poorly manicured, clad in a dress, petticoat, bra, cardigan, two vests, and another cloth fashioned into a diaper. She had also been poisoned with carbon monoxide and strangled. She, too, had been drinking before her death which was also eight to 12 weeks earlier and this victim was six months pregnant. She, again, a prostitute, was identified at Rita Nelson, 25.

The final victim—found under the floorboards—was a woman in her 50s, plump, and missing several teeth. She was rolled up in a flannel blanket with a pillowcase over her head. She was also wrapped in a flowered dress and silk nightgown and wore stockings. She had been dead approximately 12-15 weeks. She had been strangled by ligature but unlike the others there was no evidence of gas poisoning or sexual intercourse. She was identified as Ethel Christie.

Additional evidence found in the flat included potassium cyanide, a man's tie fashioned into a reef knot in the kitchen cupboard, a man's suit under floorboards of the common hallway, and a tobacco tin that contained four clumps of pubic hair; none of which belonged to any of the victims. From where Christie obtained the hair has never been resolved.

Police also found a human femur in the garden supporting a wooden trellis. Additional bones were uncovered in flowerbeds and beneath an orange blossom bush along with blackened skull bones with teeth, pieces of a dress, a newspaper fragment dated 19 July 1943, hair and teeth, and one skull. The coroner determined that there were two female corpses although only one skull had been found.

Forensic evidence enabled these last two victims to be identified as 21-year-old Ruth Margarete Fuerst who had arrived in England from Austria in 1939 and had disappeared 24 August 1943. She was around five feet seven inches with a tooth crown identified as being from Germany or Austria. When she disappeared she had been living in Notting Hill. The second victim was presumed to be Muriel Amelia Eady, 32, who had worked with Christie in a factory. The hair in Christie's garden matched hair from her former home. The black wool dress she was wearing when she disappeared matched remains in Christie's garden.

After Christie's failed affair with the woman whose husband was overseas, he didn't have any problems finding women who would, in fact, appreciate his attention. One day in a bar he met Fuerst. She worked in a factory and was also rumored to have been a prostitute. When Mrs. Christie was away she began to visit Christie at his home. One day in bed, Christie received a telegram telling him that his wife was on her way home with her brother. Christie alleged that Ruth had undressed voluntarily and asked him to have sex with her and then they could run away together. He stated that he refused and strangled her while they were having intercourse. He wrapped her in her coat and put her under the floorboards in the parlor until after his brother-in-law left and Mrs. Christie went to work. Christie then put Fuerst in the wash house and began to dig in the garden. That night he buried her in the garden. He found some of her clothing peeking up from the shallow grave and burned it.

It is hypothesized that Christie's lifelong hatred for women and repeated humiliations caused him to act the way he did. By strangling his victims he was able to exert some semblance of power and this was erotic for him as he was only able to achieve potency with women who were helpless: that being unconscious or dead. He admitted that after he killed Fuerst he experienced "a strange, peaceful thrill."

Christie met his second victim, Eady, in the company canteen as they both worked in the same factory. In October 1944 when his wife went to Sheffield to visit relatives Christie lured Eady into his house by telling her that he had a first-aid background from when he was with the War Reserve and could help her with the catarrh (mucous buildup in her nose and throat) from which she suffered. To avoid a struggle he was prepared with a contraption that resembled an inhaler with friar's balsam in a jar to mask the gas smell and a hose connected to the gas supply. Eady sat in a chair with a scarf over her head and as she inhaled, the carbon monoxide took effect; thus enabling Christie to strangle her with a stocking while simultaneously having intercourse as she was dying. He recounted experiencing the same peaceful thrill he had with Fuerst. Christie hid her body in the wash house and dug a shallow grave near the first. Later he found a broken femur bone while gardening and used it to prop up the trellis—something the police had not seen when they were investigating Timothy Evans for his wife's and daughter's murders.

Necrophilia is defined as having sexual relations with the unconscious or dead and keeping them close. There are three identified types. One is the violent variant wherein the perpetrator has an overwhelming urge to be near a corpse so they kill in order to satiate this urge. Often the individual visits the corpse where it is dumped and in some cases there is repeated sexual contact. Another type is the fantasy necrophiliac who makes death a central aspect of his or her erotic imagery. These types may ask a partner to play dead or take pictures of him or her looking dead so they can masturbate later. Christie is a textbook fantasy necrophiliac because, as mentioned, he was unable to perform absent the violence when he murdered his victims. He also had a violent necrophilia orientation in that he did, in fact, keep his victims nearby: in the alcove in his flat, under the floorboards, in his garden, and in the building's communal wash house.

Arrest

After Christie left his old flat he placed his borrowed suitcase in a locker and wandered around London. On 20 March 1953 he checked into a room at the King's Cross Rowton House with his real name and address. Despite booking seven nights he only stayed four. When a photograph of him emerged wearing his raincoat he purchased an overcoat from another man and gave him his raincoat instead. While he claimed at trial that he was in a daze, aimlessly wandering around London, his actions demonstrate that his contriving a disguise of sorts proved otherwise. He also claimed that despite news stories about corpses found at his house, he did not connect them with himself.

Out of money, Christie took to sleeping on benches and in movie theaters and was spotted by a police officer on 31 March near the Putney Embankment of the Thames River. After giving the officer a fake name and address, Christie was asked to remove his hat and was, subsequently, recognized and promptly arrested. On his being were his identification card, his Union card, an ambulance badge, a ration book, and an old newspaper clipping about the Timothy Evans trial with details about the murders.

Christie willingly gave his statement about four of his murders. He hinted that he couldn't remember something, essentially making the police "show their hand" by admitting that they did, in fact, find the two bodies in the garden. With respect to his wife Christie claimed that she had awakened him one night and she was choking; her face was blue. He tried to restore her breathing but she was suffering so badly that he got a stocking and strangled her to put her out of her misery. He then said that the bottle containing the phenobarbitone tablets he had been prescribed for insomnia was almost empty and he realized that his wife took the pills to kill herself. After leaving his dead wife in their bed for a couple of days he put her under the floorboards, admitting that he thought this was the best way to put her to rest and keep her close to him.

He managed to make the other three women's murders not his fault either. Since they were prostitutes he claimed that they were the aggressors, demanded money, and forced themselves into his flat. He claimed Nelson picked up a frying pan to hit him and they struggled and she fell into a chair "that happened to have a rope hanging from it." When Christie came to from his alleged blackout she was dead. He said he left her there overnight and in the morning—after he had a cup of tea—he wrapped her up, diapered her, and shoved her into the alcove cupboard.

With respect to Maloney, Christie said that he met her in a café and she went home with him and threatened violence and only remembers her being on the floor and that he put her into the cupboard. In reality, he gassed her, strangled her, had intercourse with her, and then diapered and wrapped her body.

Christie stated that McLennan and her boyfriend needed a place to stay so he invited them to live with him. He asked them to leave after "several uncomfortable days" and she had come back one night, struggled with Christie after he asked her leave; however, some of her clothing tore and got wrapped around her neck. He said he sat her in a chair but she appeared to be dead so he put her in the cupboard.

The numerous psychiatrists who evaluated Christie while he was in Brixton prison described him as "nauseating" and "sniveling" and he would whisper answers to questions he did not like; not unlike his demeanor during Evans' trial. He also allegedly dissociated when describing his actions, referring to himself in the third person; however, he boasted about his actions to other inmates saying that his "goal" was 12.

Trial, Conviction, and Execution

When faced with the myriad evidence against him, Christie quickly admitted to killing his first two victims but hesitated to take responsibility for Beryl Evans who he later admitted that he did, in fact, kill but not baby Geraldine. He said Beryl's was a mercy killing like his wife as a result of a botched suicide attempt on her part. Christie alleged that Beryl offered him sex to help her but he could not perform. None of the evidence corroborates Christie's account.

Christie's trial for murdering his wife commenced on 22 June 1953 at the Old Bailey. He pled not guilty by reason of insanity. His own attorney, Derek Curtis-Bennett, even called Christie a maniac and madman which was supported by Dr. Jack Abbott Hobson, a defense psychiatrist. The prosecutor's psychiatrists said that while Christie had a hysterical personality it was neurosis not a defect of reason and, therefore, Christie was not insane.

After a mere four-day trial and an 80-minute jury deliberation Christie was found guilty and sentenced to death. He did not appeal and was hanged at Pentonville Prison on 15 July 1953.

GIRL STRANGLER :

THE TRUE STORY OF SERIAL KILLER

DANA SUE GRAY

47

ERIN PIERCE

Dana Sue Gray was born on December 6th, 1957 in Pasadena, California. Her mother, Beverly Arnett, was a former beauty queen who worked as a professional model. Her father, Russell Armbrust, worked as a hairdresser and was married three times prior to marrying Beverly. The couple had several miscarriages before Dana was born.

Her mother was born for the camera and loved attention. She liked being pampered, getting her make-up done and wearing flashy outfits. Beverly modeled for Bullock's, did print ads for Hamilton watches and was once a Rose Princess at the Tournament of Roses Parade.

LIKE MOTHER LIKE DAUGHTER

Russell divorced Beverly, however, when he witnessed his wife attack an older woman that had angered her. Beverly had also maxed out his credit cards, putting him financial peril. Dana was only two years old at the time of the divorce and rarely saw her father.

"Some kind of estrangement had taken place," forensic psychologist Lora Dixon said. "After her parents divorced she had turned down invitations in her teen years to visit her father on all of the holidays and birthday get-togethers."

"There is also something to think about here in terms of Beverly's own temper. Dana clearly witnessed violence and bullying from her mother at an early age. She inherited those characteristics from her mother with tragic results."

Dana had discipline problems early on as she sought attention from her narcissistic mother. Her mother would discipline her but Dana would retaliate by stealing money to buy candy. Her mother had two other children from a previous marriage. Dana would go into the rooms of her step brothers and urinate in their beds.

Her mother would continue to try and discipline her to no avail as Dana would lash back with violence. This facet of her personality was never placed under her control.

"Mommy and daughter didn't get along," Dixon said. "But obviously that isn't unusual nor does mean she was destined to become a serial killer. There was some deep seated issues festering here though. This is evident when Dana gave her mother a snake for Christmas. 'A snake for a snake' the card must have read."

Nonetheless, it did not appear on the surface that Dana had to endure the brutal childhood that gave birth to so many other serial killers. Cedric Ward, one of her step brothers, did admit that Dana did not have the best of childhoods. "It was not happy growing up," he recalled.

SCHOOL AND SEX

Dana did not get along with other students and achieved low grades in all of her classes. She was a chronic truancy case and often forged notes to get out of class. Dara was sexually active at a very early age as she would lose her virginity at the age of twelve. She would ultimately go from one relationship to the next, using sex to lure men into her web of narcissism.

"Dana has a problem," said Richard Singer, a boyfriend of her mother. "She does not want to be told no. She has her own thing, and nobody could tell her any different. You could not tell Dana what to do."

"Her mother would pretty much try to control her, but Dana would go off on you. You could not tell her what to do. Dana is very hyperactive and opinionated."

During her adolescent years, she loved horror movies and read Grimm's Fairy Tales numerous times. As a teenager, she and a neighbor built a catapult. They would tie tiny parachutes on the cat's backs and then hurl them into the air, with the parachute carrying them down into neighborhood swimming pools.

A MOTHER'S DEATH

Beverly contracted breast cancer when Dana was fourteen. Dana decided to become a nurse after witnessing the way the nurses at the hospital treated her mother. Her mother died and Dana was forced back to live with her father.

"The temptation here is to say that Dana was inspired to become a nurse by witnessing the compassion the nurses shown her mother during her illness," Dixon said. "But I would posit a different psychological scenario. Dana saw that the nurses had power over her mother. That for once, her mother was weak and had to defer to other people for the first time in her life. Dana wanted power. Control. What better way to get that then to become a nurse?"

Dana went into a depression after her mother died and would reveal her sentimentality in letters she would write to her then boyfriend, Don Lane, in jail.

"Tomorrow, Good Friday, 4-1-94, is also April Fool's and also my real mom's 76th B-day. It's been 22 years since her death, and I still celebrate her B-day for her. I celebrate it for her 'cause she died when I was 14 and we never got to get past the 'grow years' to become friends like my dad and I are. She was wild-but made my younger years a total adventure: camping, clamming @ Pismo, best Halloween parties and the best Xmases a poor family could have. She could make a fun time out of just anything."

"Again, you see in her letters a sense of victimhood," Dixon said. "She makes no mention of her mother ignoring her birthdays. And she describes her family as 'poor.' They lived in relatively affluent area, becoming strapped for cash primarily because of Beverly's spending."

GROWING UP

Dana's father Russell had remarried, living with his new wife Yvonne who had a daughter named Cathy. Dana would move in with the couple, sharing a room with Cathy. The reunion between her and her father would be a short-lived one, however, as Yvonne would find marijuana in Dana's room.

Russell's wife then kicked Dana out of the home.

On her own at the age of fifteen, Dana would move-in with her sky-diving instructor, Rob Beaudry. The union would produce two pregnancies but Rob talked Dana in to getting abortions both times. These were decisions that she would later come to resent.

At five-foot-two and weighing a stocky 135 lbs, Dana would nonetheless inherit her mother's penchant for fancy clothes and desire to be pampered with manicures and pedicures. Despite her taste in high-end living, associates would describe her appearance and demeanor as "hard."

She would graduate from Newport High School in 1976 and enter nursing school at Saddleback College in Mission Viejo, California. Dana paid her way through nursing school while working as waitress. She also taught herself screen printing techniques and sold screen printed items for extra cash.

"Dana inherited her mother's psychology when it came to money and relationships," Dixon said. "She operated from a 'lack mindset', in that she always saw herself as poor. She was industrious but felt sorry for herself that she had to work so hard, paying her way through school and working for a living. The shopping sprees were a relief to her perceived burden."

ESTRANGED FROM FAMILY

Dana became estranged from her half-brothers, her older siblings from Beverly's previous marriage. The reasons were always financial as she become embroiled in a dispute over the proceedings from their aunt's estate.

She had run-ins with her half-brother Rick in particular.

Dana reacted with anger after he told her to sell belongings to pay her mounting bills. Rick wrote back telling her that she had no consideration for others.

"Nuts," is how her sister-in-law described her. "Not even normally greedy. Crazy. Gray is missing a conscience. I do not think it is there. When you talk to her, she has no concept of other human beings."

"The half-brothers clearly knew she was trouble," Dixon said. "They did the right thing in distancing themselves.

NURSING CAREER.

Immediately upon graduating from Saddleback, Dana landed a nursing job at Corona Community Hospital. She used that as a springboard to a high paying position as an operating room nurse at Inland Valley Regional Medical Center (some reports have her identified as a labor and delivery nurse). She was described by one nursing supervisor as "very caring."

During this time, she had found another boyfriend, a windsurfer whom she would accompany on trips to Hawaii where they would pursue various outdoor activities. This relationship would be an on-again, off-again type deal until Dana would marry Tom Gray. The couple would tie the knot at a winery in the affluent Temecula area.

Tom was an active sportsman and had a crush on Dana since high school.

"She was a hard core athlete," Tom recalled. "A sky diver, wind surfer, mountain bike enthusiast and snorkeler, and she was skilled in each sport."

Dana took pride in her physical strength and would often roll up her sleeve to reveal her bicep muscle. 'She how strong I am?' she would ask.

Living in the gated community of the affluent Canyon Lake suited Dana as it would have been something that would have pleased her mother. Her and Tom started numerous businesses where they used the name "Graymatter."

Tom could not stop Dana's spending habits, however. The couple took out a loan for $47,000 and another for $20,000 within the first nine months of their marriage.

"She was replicating the marriage of her mother and father," Dixon said. "She liked the empowerment that came from having a lot of money. Having money, or rather the act of spending money is what fed her ego. Only in Dana's case she took it way beyond her mother. She was willing to kill for that feeling."

The marriage quickly soured when Dana's spending habits sent the couple into overwhelming consumer debt. Her alcoholism also worsened, particularly after she suffered a miscarriage. Dana indulged in three or four glasses of wine while cooking dinner and then having more with the dinner itself. Her days off from the hospital were adventures in bourbon whiskey, 7-Up and Tequila shooters. Later, she would admit to using marijuana and cocaine.

When Gray unexpectedly received a $7500 inheritance, Dana took the money and blew it on a trip to Europe, leaving her husband behind at home. When she returned , she began an affair with Don Lane, a musician in her husband's band. When Lane agreed to support her, she moved out of the Canyon Lake house and spent $11,000 in five months.

In March of 1992, however, Dana began seeing a psychiatrist. He prescribed Paxil for her, probably to stave off depression among other things.

Lane had a five year old son at the time and would later tell authorities of Dana's "mood changes" and her propensity to break out into "hysterical tears" with little provocation.

She filed for divorce from Tom but this would not be finalized until much later. In September of 1993, Tom and Dana were forced to file for bankruptcy to prevent foreclosure on their Canyon Lake residence.

Despite the value of the home increasing, the amount they owed on the house was more than its worth. They owed $177,500 on a house valued at $125,000 because of double mortgages.

She suffered a miscarriage, exacerbating more depression as well as alcohol and drug abuse.

FIRED FROM THE HOSPITAL

The trouble continued for Dana as two months later she would be fired from the hospital for stealing Demerol and other opiate pain killers.

"What Dana was trying to do was medicate herself," Dixon said. "The new marriage, the exotic vacations, the fancy house and cars. It was never enough to quell the demons that spoke in her head. A control freak out of control. So she struggled to constantly fill the void with booze and drugs. Then this spirals into an affair with a friend of her husband. Again, this life trajectory happens to a lot of people. In Dana's case, however, she needed that extra thrill. Something more than the rush of sky-diving, cheating on her husband, and getting high. She needed the ultimate adrenaline rush. The power to take someone's life."

TIME TO KILL

In later reports, hospital authorities would reveal their own problems with Gray.

"She is sarcastic," Darlena Addison, the former nursing supervisor who fired Gray for stealing drugs. "She does get her point across if she's crossed or doesn't get her way."

"The problem was a condescending attitude, as Dana believed that she was smarter than everyone and had a need to dominate."

The hospital would later report that they did not have any "unusual" deaths during Gray's tenure.

"Of course that is what you would expect them to say," Dixon said. "If they admit to any 'unusual' deaths then it certainly opens them up to a lawsuit. The opportunity would certainly be there for Dana to steal credit cards from elderly patients and rack up bills. It appears, however, that she did not put her murderous impulses into action until after her dismissal. Dana fell in love with the struggle. The fight of her victim as long as she would emerge on he winning end. Poisoning her victims to death in the way it would have been possible for her as a nurse would not have given her that adrenaline rush."

After the loss of her job, Dana would amp up her indulgences in alcohol, drinking straight Vodka, loving the Smirnoff brand in particular.

On Valentine's Day in 1994, Dana contacted Tom's parents (after their separation he had kept his phone number and address a secret). She informed Tom's parents that she wanted to meet with him.

Tom agreed at first but later did not show up.

Tom would find out that Dana had taken out an insurance policy on him without his knowledge. The policy payout would have been enough to pay down the Canyon Lake home the couple used to share.

Later that day, Dana murdered Norma Davis.

THE FIRST VICTIM

Norma Davis was 86 years old at the time. She was the mother-in-law of the woman (Jeri Davis Armbrust) who married Dana's father in 1988. Jeri's first husband, Bill Davis, was Norma's son. Bill died in the early 1980s, and his widow married a newly divorced Russell.

But Jeri continued to care for her elderly mother-in-law, even after she remarried. Dana would also come to know Norma very well.

On February 16th, 1994, however, the body of Norma Davis would be found by a neighbor named Alice Williams. She had been dead for two days as someone had stabbed her in the neck with a wood-handled utility knife. The blade had been inserted so deep that it nearly severed Norma's head.

She also had a filet knife sticking out of her chest.

Police would discover no forced entry into the home. Norma always kept the doors locked unless she was expecting a visitor. Her neighbor, Alice, stated that she could not remember if Norma had mentioned she was expecting company.

"We didn't have a lot of information," Detective Joe Greco said. "The only piece of evidence that we had was the entry way of the condominium. There was a faint shoe print on the condominium and it was a 6 ½ size shoe."

Detectives would find the Nike shoe print and Davis' Social Security check in plain view. Additionally, on the first floor of the condo, they found a smear of blood on an armchair and a torn phone cord.

A modus operandi had been established. Dana would manually strangle her victims with a phone cord, then use an object to smash or stab.

The coroner concluded that Norma Davis was strangled first then stabbed. She was stabbed eleven times with Dana leaving the knives stuck in her body.

Police described the scene as one of the most brutal they had ever encountered.

"It was a shock because it was only my second homicide case as a detective," Greco said. "It was overwhelming. It crossed my mind that I had a serial killer on my hands."

SHE DEVIL ON A RAMPAGE

"The community was very affluent," Greco said. "They don't have a lot of homicides."

On February 28th, 1994, 66-year old June Roberts was found murdered. She had lived in the gated community of Canyon Lake along with Dana.

Dana had known Roberts and visited her that day saying that she wanted to borrow a book about either overcoming alcohol addiction or vitamins, the reports vary. Dana had her boyfriend's five year old son waiting out in front in her Cadillac.

Ignorant of Dana's true motives, Roberts allowed Dana into her home. She went to retrieve the book Dana inquired about while her would-be killer ripped out the cords to June's phone

Dana would later describe their interaction taking a turn when she became "really annoyed" that June came back with the wrong book. She also told a psychologist that she became infuriated that June allegedly said that she "didn't do enough" to save her marriage with Tom.

When asked what made Dana believe that Roberts and her other victims were looking down on her, Dana responded that she did not like their body language.

"The arching of the eyebrow," Dana said. "That is what happened. All three."

Dana then used the phone cord to strangle Roberts to death.

"I was right behind her," Dana recalled. "I choked her with the phone cord. She was holding on, trying to get the cord off. I pulled her down. She was on her back. I hit her in the head with a bottle. I lost it. I was so consumed. I don't know the time span in there-must have been very quick. She must have stopped moving, and I left. As I walked out, she had a little wallet thing. I grabbed it."

"We went out and proceeded to shop up a storm. "

In talking to psychologists,.Dana appeared unaware of the concept of remorse.

"It was very brutal," Greco said. "The victim had been strangled with her own telephone cord and actually tied to a chair. And she was struck so hard (by the wine bottle) she fractured her skull."

Her autopsy noted a "moderately deep ligature furrow" and a "6 x 3 purple contusion." The cranium contusion was caused by a heavy glass wine bottle striking her with tremendous force. The volume of blood in and near the bathroom door, the walls and pooling under the body made it impossible to gauge the age of the victim.

"This is when the profile of Dana Sue becomes highly unusual," Dixon said. "With female serial killers, you usually see poison or the use of a gun as the weapon of choice. Dana Sue, however, approached her victims with a high level of physical violence that rivaled a male serial killer. There was nothing lady-like about her approach. She was a cold blooded, hands on killer."

TIME TO SHOP

Dana did not hesitate after murdering Roberts, she had to get her shopping fix met.

She would go to Bally's Wine Country Cafe in Temecula, eat crab cake and scampi while charging the meal to Robert's credit card. She could not finish the entire meal, however, and had the waitress pack the rest.

She then got an eyebrow wax and a perm then treated her boyfriend's son to a stylish haircut.

"The fact that she had the little boy accompany her on both the murders and the shopping trips deserves mention," Dixon said. "Dana remained childless throughout life. She was regretted getting two abortions and suffered a miscarriage during her marriage with Tom. Going out and about with her boyfriend's son made her feel like a Mommy. She could be the Mommy that she never had, treating the young child to things she always wanted."

Dana signed "June Roberts" on the $164.76 charge at the salon. She then went to the mall and spent $511 on a black suede jacket, several pairs of cowboy boots, and then $161 on a pair of diamond earrings all charged to Roberts. Her addiction still not satiated, she went to a drug store, picking up dog treats, two bottles of Smirnoff and a toy police helicopter for the boy.

The day after, Dana loaded up on suntan lotion, got a massage at Murrieta Hot Springs resort and then went on another power shopping spree.

"She had absolutely no remorse," Dixon said. "There was no hiding out and laying low like some other wimpy male serial killer. Dana Sue was different. She killed and then she had to do the one thing that gratified her. She had to get to the mall. She had to get the high from buying stuff. She had to enjoy the power while it still lasted."

Ironically, none of her victims had anything stolen aside from their credit cards.

"Dana didn't take any rings from her victims," Greco said. "Or some valuables from the home that were obvious. So I don't think any of the crimes were motivated by money."

Ten days after the Roberts' murder, Dana would enter an antique store, the Main Street Trading Post in Lake Elsinore. Dana stated to the cashier, Dorinda Hawkins, that she wanted to buy a picture frame for a photo of her deceased mother.

"Dana came in asking about picture frames," Greco said. "During their interaction, Dana felt that Dorinda was being condescending to her.

"I felt sick to my stomach," Dana said. "I wanted to vomit. I wanted her to die."

Dana asked if Hawkins was working alone and then she attacked her, strangling her with the store's telephone cord.

"Dorinda is begging for her life when Dana is strangling her," Greco said. "And Dorinda told her 'you can have anything you want. Take the cash, I have eight kids, just let me live.' And Dana told her 'I'm not doing this for the money.' She said that twice. And that really gives you an insight on what Dana is thinking while she's committing these crimes."

Dorinda, however, continued to fight, resisting Dana all the way.

"Relax," Dana said, trying to coax Hawkins into dying. "Just relax."

Hawkins grabbed a broom and poked Dana with it to no avail.

Dana then shoved Hawkins to the ground and stepped on her head as a brace to better choke her.

"Her eyes were flat," Hawkins recalled. "I could tell she had killed before."

Believing her victim dead, Dana stole five dollars from Hawkins' purse and twenty dollars from the cash register.

An hour later, she began another shopping spree, still using Roberts' credit cards.

Hawkins, however, would survive the attack and provide the police the required description of Dana.

THE ATTACKS CONTINUE

Nearly a month after her first killing, on March 16th, 1994, Dana would kill the 87-year old Dora Beebe.

Moments after Beebe arrived home from a doctor's appointment, Dana pulled up in front of her house. She knocked on the door and asked Beebe for directions.

"Here we see Dana getting bolder," Dixon said. "With Norma Davis and June Roberts, she knew the victims beforehand. And the attempted murder in the antique store seemed to be a spur of the moment thing. But the Beebe murder is the first occasion where Dana has picked out a stranger. Elderly women were her preferred target, specifically those who were alone, and tragically Beebe emerged in her cross-hairs."

Living in the same neighborhood for several years, it was improbable for Dana to become lost. But she used that as an excuse when she came knocking on Beebe's door asking for directions.

Dana became angry when Beebe said "I don't have time for this." She was able to hide her anger as Beebe capitulated and allowed Dana insider her home to look at a map. Once inside the home, however, Dana assaulted the elderly woman.

'She turned her back on me," Dana said. "I choked her with the phone cord. I hit her in the head with an iron. As I remember it, it wasn't much of a fight."

Using a stainless steel Black and Decker iron that Dana found in the home, Dana bashed Beebe in the head so hard that it dented the appliance.

Less then an hour later, Dana would be at the mall with Beebe's credit cards in hand.

"She enjoyed doing things that were risky," Greco said. "She was a thrill seeker. I think that she really enjoyed what she was doing. She got a thrill out of it."

PANIC IN THE STREETS

The residents in the gated community of Canyon Lake went into panic mode. Some of the elderly citizens moved in with family until the killer was caught. A group of elderly widows organized themselves to sleep together at designated houses, not wanting to be alone.

There were some who thought the killings where the product of a cult engaging in the ritual sacrifice of the elderly.

"Rumors circulated around the entire community," Dixon said. "A terrifying time for everyone, the elderly in particular. This was a relatively well-to-do neighborhood. People were unused to killings, let alone a serial killer. Numerous people bought guns and kept it by their bedside while others banded together in the belief that there were safety in numbers."

FALSE SUSPECT

Police detectives were at a loss early on in finding a suspect. Prospects were so bleak that a supervisor in charge had seriously thought about using a psychic. Dana was not anywhere near the police's list of possible killers. Instead, the police initially suspected that her mother-in-law, Jeri Armbrust, might be the killer.

The police determined that Armbrust used to be married to Davis' son and continued to care for her former mother-in-law.

Detectives grew suspicious because it was unusual that Jeri would continue to take care of someone who was not a blood relative. Norma Davis herself was on death's door, recovering from a triple bypass surgery.

Police determined that Jeri had been in Davis' house the Sunday before the murder and that she wore a pair of Nike shoes.

Jeri stated that she did come to Davis' house but only came to drop off groceries. She heard the TV on upstairs but did not go up to say hello. She left the groceries on the counter and went home.

Police questioned why she didn't say hello but after weeks of questioning police determined that Jeri was not a suspect. She instead became an ally to the investigation.

CAPTURE

Descriptions obtained from the various merchants at the shopping center were eventually used to catch Dana. She had been buying so much stuff that the credit card company called June Roberts' family to inquire about the excessive spending.

Police detectives went to all of the stores where Roberts' credit card had been used, interviewing the cashiers. They obtained a physical description of Dana, surmising that the killer had dyed her hair recently and was accompanied by a little boy.

Detective Greco relayed this information to Jeri Armbrust.

Jeri surmised that the killer was in fact, her step-daughter Dana. She said that Dana recently dyed her hair red and had a boyfriend who had a young son.

Greco then obtained a search warrant and called for the aid of ARCNET (Allied Riverside County Narcotics Enforcement Team) to stake out Gray's home in Lake Elsinore.

Unfortunately, Dana was murdering Dora Beebe just hours before they determined her to be the killer. They followed Dana to a bank where she used Beebe's credit card and then went out for another shopping spree.

"We were able to follow the paper trail created by the use of these credit cards," Greco said. "With the merchants we were able to get a general description of the suspect."

Later that day, Greco arrested Dana while she was cooking dinner. Assisting officers took her boyfriend and his son in for questioning.

HOUSE OF STOLEN GOODS

Police did a thorough search of Dana's home after her arrest.

"They found jewelry, food, liquor, a ski mask, a purse with nearly $2,000 stuck in the washing machine, and many items of clothing," one report stated. "The police obtained a wealth of evidence: Gray's use of credit cards, clerks who had seen her directly after each murder, handwriting experts who identified her signatures on various items."

Dana was interrogated for hours.

"In the interview," Greco recalled. "Dana talked about finding a purse. And that purse belonged to a woman by the name of Dora Beebe. I knew that I had the right suspect in this case. But I didn't not know that on the same day we were serving her search warrant she was killing her last victim."

Dana stated that she never took the credit cards but after police revealed that they had evidence of her using them, Dana claimed that she found both Roberts' and Beebe's cards.

She maintained this story throughout the questioning. When asked why she kept the cards she said that she "had an overwhelming need to shop."

NO REMORSE, NO SYMPATHY

Dana displayed no sympathy for the victims. One psychologist noted that some of Dana's answers were like a robot answering in a manner they believed a normal human should.

After a hearing, Deputy District Attorney Richard Bentley wanted the death penalty. Dana pleaded insanity for all charges. But a witness came forward and stated that she saw Dana at Roberts' house on the day of her death, Dana quickly changed her plea to guilty and robbing and murdering two women as well as the attempted murder at the antique shop.

"At the end of the day," Dixon said. "Dana didn't want to die. When a witness came forward and said she saw Dana at the Roberts' house perhaps she knew that she was done for and would have been executed. Maybe she did not have enough confidence in her ability to pull off the insanity defense. So she struck a deal. She would plead guilty and avoid the death penalty."

Nonetheless, prosecutors were still unable to determine how Dana left the bloody crime scenes without a speck of blood on her or any sign of a struggle. All the clerks and waitresses spotted nothing out of the usual.

LIFE WITHOUT PAROLE

On October 16th, 1998, Dana Sue Gray was sentenced to life without parole.

"It's hard to find words to describe the atrocity in this case," Judge Patrick Magers said during Dana's sentencing. "The crimes were horrendous, callous and despicable."

Dana is currently jailed at the California Women's Prison in Chowchilla.

"She enjoyed the power," Dixon said. "She got addicted to the power she obtained while she killed people who were helpless to fight back. She liked watching them struggle. Liked having control over them before they died."

Jail has not seemed to bother Dana as she referred to her incarceration as her "county condo." She continues to pester her jailers to replicate her high-maintenance civilian lifestyle. She insists on a vegetarian diet and wants the use of a chiropractor. She has requested a mirror and has lobbied consistently for the return of her belongings.

Dana has drawn chilling clown faces, cobbling her paints together from M&M's candy coating, cherry drink mix, lipstick and and baby powder.

Her family came to visit her and brought her a pair of cheap Nike's. She refused them, wanting the high-end models.

Dana continues to thumb her nose at authorities as she sometimes sends collectibles to "murderablia" websites. She has sold her panties at $250, where she autographs them and writes in her prison identification number. She sells her hand tracing for $65 and a 'prison worn shirt', decorated with a drawing of a blue butterfly perched on a skeleton's hand.

"We can look back and say that she was simply psychotic," Dixon said. "And it is really easy to dismiss her killings as someone who was simply crazy violent and not read into it anymore than that. But in looking at the ages and gender of the victim, we can see the connection.

All of her victims were old enough to be her mother. So perhaps in Dana's mind she saw her victims as substitutes for her late mother with whom had a lot of anger toward. And I mean violent, aggressive anger. So when she subdued her victims with the phone cord, she would unleash a torrent of rage, smashing them with irons, stabbing them with utility knives,bashing them over the head with wine bottles. She would attack them and have flashbacks of her battles with her Mom, doing things to the victim that she was powerless to do to her mother as a little girl."

"She was doing it all for Mommy."

THE HILLSIDE STRANGLERS

67

NAOMI ROBERTS

Cousins Kenneth Bianchi and Angelo Buono, Jr. are collectively known by their media epithet "The Hillside Strangler". These two men were responsible for the murders of at least nine females, ages 12 to 28, during the late 1970s in Los Angeles, California, and Bianchi killed two more in Washington. After their first three victims did not gain much attention because they were prostitutes, Bianchi and Buono decided to abduct and murder middle-class "nice" girls. Five victims were found on hillsides in the Glendale-Highland Park area during Thanksgiving weekend in 1977 and the resulting panic led to the coining of the moniker "Hillside Strangler".

Lead Los Angeles Police Department homicide investigator Detective Sergeant Bob Grogan, along with his partner Dudley Varney as well as Los Angeles Sheriff's Department's Detective Frank Salerno, believed that the murders were the work of more than one killer but figured the less the murderers knew about what police knew the better.

Bianchi later moved to Washington where he murdered two more women before being caught.

Both Bianchi and Buono were convicted of multiple counts of first-degree murder and sentenced to life. Buono dies of a heart attack on 21 September 2002 while serving his time in Calipatria State Prison in Calipatria, California. Bianchi continues to serve his sentence at Washington State Penitentiary in Walla Walla.

Early Lives

Kenneth Bianchi

Kenneth Alessio Bianchi was born on 22 May 1951 in Rochester, New York, to a 17-year-old alcoholic prostitute who gave him up for adoption two weeks after he was born. He was adopted by Nicholas Bianchi and Frances Sciolono and despite a stable upbringing, Bianchi became a pathological liar at a very early age. Further, as a result of petit mal seizures he suffered at the age of five, Bianchi often daydreamt as if he were in a trance.

Bianchi suffered from insomnia and frequently wet the bed as a child (one of the triad symptoms of serial killers). Frances took him to the doctor on multiple occasions for his urination problem and being examined by the doctor caused Bianchi much embarrassment and humiliation. He also had a bad temper and was diagnosed with passive-aggressive personality disorder which is characterized by an individual who may appear to be enthusiastic about and actively comply with others' desires and needs while simultaneously resisting them, thus resulting in increased anger and hostility. At the core of this disorder is that the sufferer resents responsibility and instead of openly expressing his or her feelings, demonstrates said resentment through actions such as procrastination, forgetfulness, and inefficiency. Despite having a rather high IQ of 116, Bianchi was a chronic underachiever in school. When Frances took him to a psychologist, it was determined that Bianchi was overly dependent upon his mother.

On 2 January 1957, Bianchi fell off of a jungle gym and landed on his face. His mother then sent him to a private Catholic elementary school where he excelled in creative writing. In July 1963, Bianchi pulled down a six-year-old girl's pants after "spontaneously decid[ing] that he liked doing so".

His adoptive father died in 1964, thus leaving an unemotional Bianchi having to attend public high school where he joined a motorcycle club and dated frequently. His adoptive mother was forced to work and she was known for keeping Bianchi home from school for extended periods of time.

While in high school, Bianchi set high standards for his many girlfriends such as complete fidelity and outwardly absolute devotion; however, these standard did not apply to him.

He graduated in 1971 from Gates-Chili High School in Rochester and, soon after, married his high school sweetheart, Brenda Beck; however, the couple divorced after only eight months. Rumor has it that Brenda left without a word.

Bianchi enrolled at Monroe Community College to study police science and psychology after deciding that he wanted to become a police officer; however, after only one term he dropped out and then was rejected for several positions both in Rochester and, later, Los Angeles. Consequently, Bianchi worked a series of menial odd jobs, eventually becoming a jewelry store security guard for which he was fired for stealing and giving his girlfriends the stolen jewelry. He would steal from other employers over the years.

He then left Rochester and moved to Los Angeles in late 1975 at the age of 26.

Angelo Buono, Jr.

Angelo Anthony Buono, Jr. was born on 5 October 1934, also in Rochester, New York, to first-generation Italian-American immigrants originally from San Buono, Italy. His parents divorced when he was young and a five-year-old Buono moved to Glendale, California, with his mother Jenny and his sister Cecilia, where his mother supported the family by doing piecework in a shoe factory. Raised Catholic, this had no effect on Buono's development as a decent human being.

Buono displayed a very high interest in sex from a young age and when he was a teenager claimed that he had raped and sodomized number of girls. Buono idealized serial rapist Caryl Chessman, also known as "The Red Light Bandit", calling Chessman his hero but added that Chessman should have murdered his victims. He developed a deep loathing of women and desire to injure and humiliate them, including his mother who he would verbally abuse; however, he was emotionally tied to her until her death in 1978.

Buono began stealing cars and was sent to the Paso Robles School for Boys.

In 1955, Buono married his high-school sweetheart, Geraldine Vinal, who was 17 years old at the time, who he had impregnated; however, less than a week later he left her. She would later give birth to a son, Michael Lee Buono, on 10 January 1956. Buono filed for divorce and refused to pay child support or let his son call him "Dad". He was back in jail for car theft when his first son was born.

Later, he impregnated Mary Castillo who gave birth to his second son, Angelo Anthony Buono III, at the end of 1956 and then married her in 1957. The couple would have four more children: Peter in 1957, Danny in 1958, Louis in 1960, and Grace in 1962. In 1964, Buono was believed to have sexually assaulted his two-year-old daughter Grace; however, there is insufficient literature to know fully the circumstances of the allegation. Buono's second marriage to Castillo also ended in divorce that same year after she purported that he had been physically, emotionally, and sexually abusive toward her. In a last-ditch effort to reconcile with him, Castillo was "rewarded" with his handcuffing her and threatening to kill her at gunpoint. Castillo would later recount a night during the first year they were together where Buono tied her spread-eagled to the bedposts and "raped her so violently she was afraid that he was going to kill her" and "her pain seemed to him his greatest pleasure" and, thus, he had no qualms of hurting her and didn't seem to care that the children witnessed the abuse. He avoided paying child support again.

Buono married a third time in 1965 to a 25-year-old single mother named Nannette Campino and the couple had two children of their own: Tony in 1967 and Sam in 1969. Despite being treated as poorly as Mary Castillo had been, Campino feared for her life on a daily basis but stayed until he began to sexually abuse her 14-year-old daughter. Buono allegedly bragged that he raped his stepdaughter because "[s]he needs breaking in" and then turned her over to his sons for their pleasure. Campino finally took her children, filed for divorce, and fled the state in 1971.

Buono, again, was arrested for auto theft and was sentenced to one year in prison; however, due to his large family his sentence was suspended so he could work to support them.

Buono married yet again, on a whim, to a woman named Deborah Taylor; however, the couple did not live together, nor did they ever divorce.

In 1975, he became a car upholsterer and purchased his own place at 703 E. Colorado Street to live and work. Despite his abuse, cockiness, overbearing nature, and lack of good looks, Buono was considered very attractive by women, particularly younger ones who were usually naïve about sex so it was easy to convince them that his outrageous demands and proclivities were normal. Thus, he frequently forced women to engage in sex acts with him and began a relationship with a teenage girl whom he twice impregnated.

He was ugly inside and out; very coarse, vulgar, ignorant, selfish, and sadistic.

Bianchi and Buono Together

At the age of 41, Buono came into contact with his cousin Kenneth Bianchi, the latter who, in 1975, moved to California and in with his cousin. Bianchi found his older cousin with "dyed black hair, gold chains around his neck, a large gaudy turquoise ring on his finger, red silk underwear and a virtual harem of jailbait girls". Buono taught Bianchi how to use fake police badges in order to coerce free sex from prostitutes. When they needed money the two also became pimps for a short time until the two girls who worked for them—Sabra Hannan and Becky Spears—escaped after enduring relentless abuse by Buono. Bianchi, still desiring to become a police officer, applied for jobs at the Los Angeles Sheriff's and Glendale Police Departments but neither were hiring. He then procured employment with a title company and used his first paycheck on an apartment and a Cadillac, moving in with coworker Kelli Boyd. Boyd rejected his marriage proposal as she considered Bianchi to be very jealous, immature, and a liar; however, in May 1977 she told him she was expecting their first child together. The couple moved to an apartment at 1950 Tamarind Avenue in Hollywood.

Bianchi also rented some office space and set himself up as a psychologist with a fake degree and credentials. He did not have many clients and when Boyd found out she was outraged. During the "Hillside Strangler" investigation, Bianchi told Boyd he had lung cancer and was undergoing chemotherapy and radiation to explain for his work absences; however, this was a lie. One day, detectives came to his apartment to ask questions but were "favorably impressed" and did not consider him a suspect at that time.

The Murders

In October 1977, the two men committed their first murder together. Their M.O. was to cruise around Los Angeles and use fake badges to convince women that they were undercover police officers. After persuading them into Buono's car that the men said was an unmarked police car, the two would take their victims to Buono's house where they would rape, torture, and strangle them with their "signature" weapon—a garrote (a handheld ligature such as a chain, rope, or strap)—although some of their victims were reportedly killed by lethal injection, electric shock, and gas asphyxiation. Their bodies were thus disposed of outside, frequently in hilly areas.

Yolanda Washington, 19

19-year-old tall, leggy, African-American prostitute Yolanda Washington disappeared on 17 October 1977 from Cathedral City, California. She was found the next day dumped just outside Forest Lawn Cemetery, beaten, raped, and strangled with a piece of cloth. Her corpse was cleaned and there were faint marks around her wrists, ankles, and neck. Her body was posed in a grotesque sexual position.

Judith Lynn Miller, 15

On 31 October, 15-year-old Judith Lynn Miller, a runaway, was found in a La Crescenta-Montrose neighborhood, face up on a parkway in a residential area. The homeowner covered her with a tarp so that neighborhood children wouldn't see her. After the incident, that same homeowner relocated his family to another state.

The victim was small and thin, perhaps 90 pounds, with medium length reddish-brown hair. She had bruising around her neck. She had also been raped and sodomized and her body had been posed with her legs in a diamond-like position.

Los Angeles Sheriff's Department Sergeant Frank Salerno was called to the site. He noticed insect activity upon her skin and on her eyelid was "a small piece of light-colored fluff" that he saved for forensic experts. He surmised that she had been killed elsewhere and her body had been deliberately placed where it would quickly be found.

At her autopsy, the coroner determined that she had been killed around midnight and was raped and sodomized.

There was no missing person's report matching this latest victim so after a couple of days, Salerno had the newspapers run a small story on her with a request to contact the police if anyone could identify her. Still nothing. Salerno then took her picture to Hollywood Boulevard and showed it to hundreds of runaways, addicts, homeless people, and prostitutes. The name Judy Miller kept coming up as a young destitute prostitute. One man named Markust Camden—a self-proclaimed bounty hunter—told Salerno that he saw Judy Miller leave the local fish and chips restaurant at 9:00 p.m. the night before she was found dead. In fact, he would pick Buono out of a police photo lineup, but failed to recognize Bianchi.

Eventually, Salerno was able to track down the Miller family and got a positive identification. They had nothing useful to contribute to the investigation.

Elissa "Lissa" Teresa Kastin, 21

Lissa Kastin, 21, was working as a waitress at the Healthfaire Restaurant to pay for ballet lessons as she was an avid dancer. She also worked part time for her father's real estate and construction business. She was last seen leaving work the night of 5 November. She was found the next day near the Chevy Chase Country Club in Glendale on 6

November; which was also near to where Buono lived. She had been beaten, raped, and strangled to death.

Salerno compared notes with the Glendale Police Department and noticed similarities between his latest victim and this new one. Both bodies had the same five-point ligature marks—ankles, wrists, and neck—and had been dumped within six miles of each other. This latest victim had been raped but there was no evidence of sodomy.

When Salerno looked at the dump site he was confident that at least two men were involved due to the large guardrail between the street and where the body was found and the near impossibility that one man could have gotten her body over it alone.

Dolores Cepeda, 12 and Sonja Johnson, 14

After their early murders failed to attract much publicity, Bianchi and Buono decided to find some younger victims.

12-year-old Dolores Cepeda and 14-year-old Sonja Johnson were abducted in Highland Park, California, on 13 November. They had last been seen getting off a school bus heading home from St. Ignatius School and approaching a large two-tone sedan that, reportedly, had two men inside.

Both young girls were found on 20 November in the hills between Glendale and Eagle Rock, near Dodger Stadium by a young nine-year-old boy who was treasure hunting in the trash on the hillside.

Los Angeles Police Department Homicide Detective Dudley Varney had been called to this site.

Kristina Weckler, 20

That same day, 20-year-old Kristina Weckler was found on the other side of the same hillside where Cepeda and Johnson were found.

Weckler was a quiet, loving, and serious honors student at the Pasadena Art Center of Design and lived in Glendale.

She was found nude, raped, tortured, and strangled to death as evidenced by ligature marks on her neck, as well as around her wrists and ankles. She had blood oozing from her rectum and bruises on her breasts. Weckler was the first victim to show additional overt signs of torture; having been injected with Windex glass cleaner she had oozing injection marks on her arms.

Los Angeles Police Department Homicide Detective Sergeant Bob Grogan—Varney's partner—was called to this site. He noticed that there was no indication of any disturbance of the foliage in the area or evidence that the body had been dragged there. Grogan made a mental note that she likely had been killed elsewhere and then carried and dumped in this location by one or maybe two men.

At this point, police were entertaining the idea that there was more than one killer and that they were becoming increasingly more sadistic.

Jane Evelyn King, 28

28-year-old actress Jane King disappeared in Los Angeles around 10 November 1977, and was found near the Los Feliz off ramp of the Golden State Freeway on 23 November. She had been sodomized and strangled and her body was badly decomposed. After King was found, Los Angeles Police Department officials—in addition to Glendale Police Department and Los Angeles County Sheriff's Department officers—created a task force to catch the "Hillside Strangler".

Lauren Rae Wagner, 18

18-year-old student Lauren Wagner lived with her parents in the San Fernando Valley. Her parents had gone to bed on 28 November, expecting their daughter to return home before midnight. The next morning, they found her car parked across the street with the door ajar.

Wagner was found later that day in a wooded area near Glendale's Mount Washington area. She was lying partially in the street, nude, with ligature marks on her ankles, wrists, and neck. Wagner, too, had been tortured as the palms of her hands contained several burn marks.

At the dump site was also a "shiny track of some sticky liquid, which had attracted a convoy of ants". Police considered that if the substance was saliva or semen from the killer then, perhaps, his blood type could be determined, as tests on semen found inside the earlier victims revealed nothing. It was later found that Bianchi was not a secretor, in that his blood type could not be determined by other bodily fluids. DNA testing had not come into popularity at this time.

When Wagner's father questioned the neighbors, it turned out that the woman who lived in the house where his daughter's car was parked, Beulah Stofer, saw Wagner's abduction. Stofer said that Wagner had pulled over to the curb at around 9:00 p.m. and two men had parked their car beside hers. After some type of disagreement, Wagner "ended up in the car with the two men".

When Grogan went to talk to the neighbor, she told him that she had just had a phone call from a man with a New York accent who told her to "keep her mouth shut about what she had witnessed or he would kill her". Stofer also told Grogan that the car was a large dark sedan with a white top and that one of the men dragged Wagner from her car into his while Wagner protested, "You won't get away with this!" Stofer described one man as tall and young with acne scars while the other was older and shorter, Latin-looking, and with bushy hair. She said she was positive that she would identify them again. This statement rang true when she picked both Bianchi and Buono out of a photo lineup shown to her by Grogan.

Kimberly Diane Martin, 17

Tall, blonde prostitute Kimberly Martin, 17, disappeared from Echo Park, California, and was found strangled to death on 13 December 1977 on a steep hillside on Alvarado Street. Martin had worked for the Climax "modeling agency".

Police believed they had two reasonably good leads in this case. First, Martin's last "client" called her to 1950 Tamarind, apartment 114; however, this turned out to be a vacant apartment. Secondly, the murderer called from a payphone in the lobby of the Hollywood Public Library on Ivar Street. Unfortunately, nothing came from these leads.

Cindy Lee Hudspeth, 20

On 16 February 1978, 20-year-old Bible school teacher and secretary at an Echo Park church Cindy Hudspeth was found in the trunk of her bright orange 1977 Datsun B210 that had been pushed over a cliff on Angeles Crest in Los Angeles National Forest near La Canada. She had been raped and strangled, with the strangulation marks similar to those associated with the "Hillside Strangler".

Hudspeth was also a neighbor of Weckler even though the two women did not know each other. Interestingly, Bianchi also lived in the same apartment complex; however, this lead was never pursued even though both Grogan and Salerno believed that there was a good chance that at least one of the murderers lived in the Glendale area.

After this case, the lack of additional victims resulted in the disbanding of the "Hillside Strangler" Task Force.

Jill Barcomb, 18 (originally believed to be a Hillside Strangler victim)

18-year-old prostitute Jill Barcomb was abducted in Beverly Hills and found near the famous Hollywood sign on 9 November. Whereas it was originally believed that she was a victim of the "Hillside Strangler" because she had been raped, beaten, and strangled, in 2005, her death was conclusively proven through DNA analysis to have been committed by Rodney Alcala, the "Dating Game Killer".

Also, sometime in 1977, the two men gave Catharine Lorre a ride with the intent of killing her; however, when they learned that she was the daughter of famous actor Peter Lorre who played a child murderer in Fritz Lang's 1931 masterpiece film *M*, they let her go. She had no idea who the men were until they were arrested.

The two stopped killing after their ninth victim, Hudspeth (although at this time it was presumed they had ten victims with Barcomb), likely due to the birth of Bianchi's son and, as some surmise, that he had made some acquaintances within the Los Angeles Police Department who would take him on ride-alongs around the city, ironically, looking for the killers, and Bianchi could talk about nothing else while in police presence. On the night they had tried to abduct another victim, the two men got into a heated argument when Bianchi told his cousin that he had been questioned in the "Hillside Strangler" case. After Bianchi's confession about being questioned by police, Buono, furious, threatened to kill his cousin.

Bianchi's Washington Murders

Bianchi's girlfriend, Kelli Boyd gave birth to their son, Sean, in February 1978, and in March Boyd decided to return to her parents in Bellingham, Washington, as she was tired of both Los Angeles and Bianchi's lifestyle. After three months of pleading to be reunited, Boyd relented and Bianchi moved to Washington in May. Bianchi's role as boyfriend and father was relatively successful and he even took a job as a security guard, ultimately earning the trust of his supervisors. However, this way of life did little to alleviate Bianchi's murderous urges. Within six months he was actively looking for new victims.

On 11 January 1978, Bianchi lured two Western Washington University students—roommates Karen Mandic, 22, and Diane Wilder, 27—to a house he allegedly "guarded" under the pretense of housesitting. Once there, he raped, tortured, and murdered them.

On 12 January, police were informed that two female students were missing after Mandic's boss became worried that she didn't arrive at work that day. He did remember that she had told him she had accepted a housesitting job in a wealthy Bayside neighborhood from a security guard friend of hers. When former-priest-turned-Bellingham-Police-Chief Terry Mangan went to the girls' home he found a hungry cat, as well as the address of the home where they were to housesit. The name of one security guard kept coming up, as well as a record that Bianchi had used a company truck that same night, supposedly to take into the shop for repairs. This never happened. Mangan began to consider the fact that the women had met with foul play.

Police then went to the Bayside house and found a wet footprint. They also interviewed a neighbor who told them that a security guard asked her to check on the house except for the night the women disappeared because "there was special work being done to the alarm system and he didn't want her to be taken as an intruder".

After a press conference, a woman called police to report that a car had been abandoned near her home in a heavily-wooded area. In the car were the bodies of Mandic and Wilder. Both had bruising and had been strangled to death.

Mangan had the security guard picked up. He gave them no trouble. His name was Kenneth Bianchi.

There was ample forensic evidence in this case; most notably foreign pubic hairs on the girls and fibers from the house's carpet matching fibers on the dead girls' clothing and shoes. Additionally, when police searched Bianchi's home they found several items stolen from job sites where he worked.

Remembering back to the "Hillside Strangler" cases in Los Angeles—and knowing Bianchi had lived there—Mangan called the police departments in California who had worked on the task force. He spoke to Detective Frank Salerno to whom everything finally made sense. Detectives tirelessly worked to link Bianchi to the strangler cases and were confident that he was one of the murderers.

Investigation and Arrest

Bianchi was not as careful this time, having left significant clues, most notably his car with California license plates was seen and subsequently connected to the addresses of two Hillside Strangler victims. Without mastermind Buono, Bianchi didn't have the wherewithal to cover his tracks.

Bianchi was arrested the following day, on 12 January 1979.

Buono was arrested on 22 October 1979, after Bianchi told police about his cousin's complicity in the murders.

Trial and Conviction

Prior to his 1981 trial, Bianchi decided to plead not guilty by reason of insanity and claimed to have a separate personality named

"Steve Walker" who had committed the murders. After several interviews by experts specializing in multiple personality disorder and hypnosis, it was determined that he was faking. Immediately after Dr. Martin Orne mentioned to Bianchi that in genuine cases of multiple personality disorder there are typically at least three personalities, Bianchi created another alter ego named "Billy", shortly followed by two more. It was later determined that the name "Steven Walker" came from a student whose identity Bianchi had previously tried to steal to enable him to fraudulently practice psychology. Further, in Bianchi's apartment investigators found several psychology books which laid credence to Bianchi's ability to fake the disorder. He was eventually diagnosed with antisocial personality disorder with sexual sadism.

During trial, there was significant physical trace evidence against the two men; including fibers from Buono's upholstery from his home and workshop on two of the victims; an imprint of a fake police badge on his wallet; and hairs from rabbits he had raised on another victim.

Bianchi agreed to plead guilty and testify against his cousin in order to get leniency, albeit uncooperatively (evidence of his passive-aggressive personality disorder).

Judge Ronald M. George—who would later become California Supreme Court Chief Justice—said during Buono's sentencing hearing, "I would not have the slightest reluctance to impose the death penalty in this case were it within my power to do so. Ironically, although these two defendants utilized almost every form of legalized execution against their victims, the defendants have escaped any form of capital punishment." On an interesting side note, George's roommate at the time was author Darcy O'Brien who, four years after the trial, wrote a book about the case.

Both men were sentenced to life in prison.

While incarcerated, Buono married mother-of-three Christine Kizuka in 1986 while she was visiting her husband—and father of her children—who was in the cell next door to Buono at the Los Angeles

County Jail, serving 18 months for assault with a deadly weapon. She worked as a supervisor at the California State Employment Development Department.

Whereas the 64-year-old Bianchi continues to serve his life sentence at the Washington State Penitentiary in Walla Walla, Buono died of a heart attack on 21 September 2002 while serving life at Calipatria State Prison in Calipatria, California. Denied for parole on 18 August 2010, Bianchi will next be eligible for parole in 2025.

Aftermath

Bianchi is also a suspect in the "Alphabet Murders"—also known as the "Double Initial Murders"—which occurred in the early 1970s in his hometown of Rochester wherein three young girls were raped, strangled to death, and dumped in the wilderness. At the time he worked as an ice cream vendor situated near two of the murder sites. On 16 November 1971, ten-year-old Carmen Colon disappeared and was found two days later in Churchville, New York, 12 miles from where she was last seen. 11-year-old Wanda Walkowicz disappeared on 2 April 1973 and was found the next day in Webster, New York, off State Route 104, seven miles from Rochester. Finally, on 26 November 1973, Michelle Maenza, 11, disappeared and was found two days later in Macedon, New York, a mere 15 miles from Rochester. They were called the "Alphabet Murders" because not only did the young victims have the same initial for their first and last name but they were also found in cities which began with the same letter.

Whereas Bianchi has repeatedly tried to get his name cleared from these murders he remains a suspect because his vehicle was seen near two of the murder sites.

Another series of murders with similar circumstances occurred in California in the late 1970s and investigators have hypothesized that they are connected to the Rochester "Alphabet Murders". In 1977, Roxene Roggasch, Paula Parsons, and Carmen Colon (like one of the original "Alphabet Murder" victims) were found raped and dead.

Whereas Bianchi was tried for six murders, DNA exonerated him of the California "Alphabet Murders".

A 2008 movie entitled *The Alphabet Killer* was very loosely based upon the murders, and in 2010 a book written by Cheri Farnsworth called *Alphabet Killer: The True Story of the Double Initial Murders* was released.

In 1980, Bianchi started a relationship with a Veronica Lynn Compton, who was a defense witness during his trial. Compton, a cocaine addict who was fascinated by serial killers, was working as a scriptwriter in Hollywood. On one of her numerous visits with Bianchi while he was incarcerated, she gave him a copy of her screenplay entitled *The Mutilated Cutter*, about a female serial killer, and asked for this input. Compton grew increasingly fixated and allegedly fell in love with Bianchi. Later, she was convicted and incarcerated for attempting to strangle a cocktail waitress who she had lured to a hotel in a ploy to have the world—and authorities—believe that the real "Hillside Strangler" was still on the loose and that the wrong man was incarcerated. To make it look like an authentic "Hillside Strangler" murder, Bianchi manipulated and used Compton as a means to get out of prison by giving her semen of his smuggled out of the facility in a rubber glove to plant on the body. Despite that DNA forensics had not been utilized at that time, semen could still be analyzed to demonstrate the killer's blood type; however, Bianchi was not a secretor. The intended victim managed to get away and Compton was tried and convicted of first-degree attempted murder and sentenced to life. Compton was paroled from prison in 2003.

In 1992, Bianchi sued Catherine Yronwode for $8.5 million for putting an image of his face on a trading card. He claimed his face was his trademark. The case was dismissed with the judge saying that if Bianchi's face was, indeed, his trademark during the murders then he would not have tried to hide it from police.

In 2007, Buono's grandson, Christopher Buono, shot his grandmother—Mary Castillo who was married to Buono at one time—and then committed suicide. Christopher was unaware of his grandfather's true identity until 2005.

Bianchi and Buono are immortalized in film. The 1989 film *The Case of the Hillside Stranglers*—based on O'Brien's book—starred Dennis Farina as Buono and Billy Zane as Bianchi. In the 2004 film *The Hillside Strangler*, Buono was portrayed by actor Nicholas Turturro and Bianchi was portrayed by C. Thomas Howell.

The 2006 movie *Rampage: The Hillside Strangler Murders* starred Tomas Arana as Buono and Clifton Collins, Jr. as Bianchi.

In 2001 the Discovery Channel aired an episode of *The New Detectives* that revisited the murders.

Bianchi and Buono have also been mentioned several times on the television show *Criminal Minds* as an example of killer teams with psychopathic predatory sexual sadist personalities who murdered their victims together.

ROADSIDE STRANGLER

85

JASMINE GREY

When one envisions a serial killer, they think of a cold, calculating, heartless monster. As humans, some of us have developed ways to recognize other humans that are looking to cause us harm. If we look at a mug shot of famous another serial killer, like Charles Manson or Jeffery Dahmer, one could say that these men "look" like serial killers. Maybe it's because of their wild eyes, the way that they hold themselves, or the "creepy" feeling one receives from their presence. These factors are enough to make a person stay as far away from the killer as possible, but sadly, not all predators come with a warning sign. Michael Bruce Ross, later to be known as the Roadside Strangler, was a ruthless predator that slipped under the radars of the multiple women that he attacked, raped, and murdered. Detective Malchik, Ross' arresting officer, described this serial killer as, "There was nothing threatening about him, there was no signal to any of these people that there was a dark side or something that they should be afraid of. He was able to conceal that until it became time for him to attack these innocent, young women." Ross seemed to be an average-looking man of completely average-strength and abilities, but underneath his calm and normal exterior beat the heart of a man who struggled with his sadistic, sexual compulsions. When someone spoke to Michael Ross, they would say that he put off a very friendly and articulate demeanor seemed very well educated and kind, but it was merely a costume that he had created over a lifetime. The creepy part about Michael Ross, despite how honest and upfront he is about his murders, is the mystery behind his words. Is he being genuine or is this merely an act? Is he being honest or are we being deceived? His state of mind drifts from monotone claims to not possess any remorse for his monstrosities to genuine pleas for a chemical castration to reduce his perverse sexual desires. Michael Bruce Ross' case was a strange one, to say the least, and his mental condition will forever be remembered as a very dark part in Connecticut history.

The Childhood

Michael Bruce Ross was born on July 26, 1959. Among three other children, Michael Bruce Ross was born into the life of a middle-class chicken farmer. His mother Pat was impregnated in high school and forced into a shotgun marriage with Michael's father, Dan Ross. Needless to say, they did not go on to lead a very happy marriage. Pat Ross was a very mentally unstable woman, who underwent two abortions and was institutionalized twice. She abandoned her children and family once to run off with another man, but she soon returned to a depressing and emotionally unhealthy life on the farm. Pat Ross seemed to resent Michael more than the other children. His sister claimed that Michael received the brunt of their mother's aggression. Michael Ross claimed that he didn't remember his dark childhood or his emotional abuse-ridden family; he only had fond memories of working on his father's farm. The joyous memories of working on the farm centered on his peculiar job; Michael's job was to ring the necks of sick and malnourished chickens.

He recalled that he began to experience sexual fantasies around this time, like most boys his age, but they weren't anything like the hellish compulsions he faced in his adulthood. He explained his boyish daydreams as non-violent, although they might've been considered peculiar by most. In an interview, Michael describes his early, innocent fantasies of women, "I would kidnap women and take them to my safe place, and then they would fall in love with me, and never want to leave." It has been said that Michael was molested as a child by his mentally ill uncle while babysitting. As an adult, Michael Ross claimed that he did not remember this incident or his uncle at all; Michael was only six years old when the suspected uncle committed suicide. Whether Michael was too young to recall the incident or if he merely repressed the memory, the irreparable damage that comes along with molestation could be a very influential part of Michael's slip into sexual sadism. Despite his strange desires, his dysfunctional family, and his history of abuse, Michael was considered to be a pretty average child. As a teenager, he excelled in school, graduating as number sixteen in his high school class, and he eventually moved to Cornell University to study Agriculture and Life Sciences.

College Years

He continued to excel academically throughout his years at university. He studied Economics, Agriculture, and Life Sciences, and excelled in all of his academic endeavors. He joined the FFA (Future Farmers of America) and the Alpha Zeta fraternity. Ross' sophomore year roommate and Alpha Zeta brother, described Ross in 1977, "He kind of followed his own drum and went his own way." Michael never made any real connections in his fraternity, nor did he really make connections to anyone besides the long string of girls that he dated. In his college year, Michael Ross was rarely without a girlfriend, and he was rarely thinking about anything but. "There was always a certain obsession on his part regarding women," said his Alpha Zeta roommate, "That seemed to be such a big issue, a constant topic—needing a woman, needing to have a girlfriend. He would be obsessed about the relationship."

Ross claims that he did not experience truly violent sexual fantasies until his years at Cornell University. He especially did not begin to fantasize about raping women until his sophomore year in college. Michael Ross said that somewhere in his undergraduate years, he began to embrace the desires that brewed within him. He started his downward spiral with a very small step. He began to stalk his fellow students on campus. He would follow close by, making it known that he was behind her. "I would get a thrill by them knowing that I was following them. That they would be scared and that gave me a thrill," Michael explained his early experimentation with his predatory nature. When simply stalking the women wasn't enough, Michael eventually turned to towards rape. He hid in the bushes of Beebe Lake and raped a visiting student. Later, he attempted to rape another girl outside of the school observatory but failed. These assaults were only stepping stones to the full-fledged horror that Michael Ross was destined to cause. During his senior year at Cornell University, Michael Ross met Dzung Ngoc Tu, a Vietnamese student, and his very first murder victim.

The case of Dzung Ngoc Tu perplexed officials everywhere. She was found on May 17, 1981, in the Fall Creek Gorge. She died from a skull fracture and her body laid there for five days until she was discovered. It appeared to be a suicide, as if she had jumped from the bridge overhead and hit her head upon the fall, but there was no suicide note left at the scene. Close friends and family of Dzung Ngoc Tu claimed that there absolutely no signs of suicidal tendencies when she was alive and investigators found absolutely no reason for killing herself. Her body showed no signs of sexual abuse, there were no suspects, and the police had no idea that the culprit was actually Michael Ross, a man who was only connected to her by their similar majors. The case went cold when the police couldn't find a suspect. It wasn't until Michael Ross was already in prison for the murders and rapes of four other women when he confessed to murdering and raping a Vietnamese girl that went to his school in New York.

The Attacks and Murders of The Roadside Strangler

Michael Ross chose his victims merely off of chance and circumstance. If he encountered a woman that was in a vulnerable position, he felt this undeniable compulsion to attack. "There's nothing they could've said or done. It was me, it wasn't them," Michael Ross admitted with a solemn tone of voice, years after his final attack, "They were dead as soon as I saw them, I think."

Michael claimed that he only attacked women to relieve pressure that built up from his personal relationships with the women in his life. When he was working in North Carolina, shortly after he graduated from college, Michael recalled that he had a very difficult visit from his fiancé, which caused him to attack a random woman shortly after he dropped his fiancé off at the airport. He noticed a woman walking on the sidewalk with a baby stroller, so Michael pulled the car over and attacked her, using her own child as a weapon. "I told her that if she didn't do what I wanted, I would smash the baby's head against the wall of the house," Michael described in an interview, he seemed as if he were on the verge of tears, "I've always said that I never understood why these women never really resisted me. I'm not a big, strong guy, but nobody ever seemed to fight. I've always just contributed it as I must say something like that, or similar to it, to the other victims." He raped and strangled the woman, then left her for dead in her driveway.

On June 15, 1982, a 23-year-old woman named Debra Smith Taylor was attacked by Michael Ross in a park. He pulled her over where no one could see them, raped her, and forced her to roll over on her stomach; he then strangled her from behind. The young girl's body was discovered much later in a dried up river bed, only a few miles away from the location of another of Ross' victims, Tammy L. Williams. "Each time I killed, I made myself believe that I wasn't going to kill again," Michael Ross explained in an interview. It wasn't very long before he killed again.

His next attack occurred on a cold Thanksgiving Day in 1983. Michael Ross encountered Robin Stavinsky outside of Norwich State Hospital. He saw the woman in a vulnerable position and he took advantage of the situation. He forced the 19-year-old girl into a wooded area and demanded her to remove her clothing. Ross forced himself on the young girl then told her to roll over on her stomach. He strangled her from behind until the innocent Robin Stavinksky died in his hands. "Serial killers like to strangle their victims and that is, I guess, the most common form of killing because there's more of a connection there. It's more real and it's not as quick," Michael Ross explained why he enjoyed strangling so much. After he was finished with her, he covered her body with leaves and left her for dead.

The Roadside Strangler struck again on Easter Sunday, 1984. April Brunias and Leslie Shelly were hitchhiking on the side of the road when Michael Ross happened to drive their way. He pulled over and offered the young girls a ride. The girls did not find Ross threatening so they got into his car and asked him to drop them off at the next gas station. When Michael passed the gas station, one of the girls drew a kitchen knife and threatened to stab him. In an interview Michael Ross explained what happened next, "I almost drove off of the road, I was so surprised. I don't know what I said, but I said something and she gave the knife to me. It obviously scared her." He parked the car at Beach Pond and used a cloth to bound both of the girls by their hands and feet. He put Leslie Shelly in the trunk of his car, then dragged the girl named April a few feet away from the car. He raped the young girl, flipped her over onto her stomach, and strangled her until she died. He then took Leslie out of the trunk and did the same thing to her. "The smallest one, Leslie Shelly, has always bothered me more than the others. I think it was because she was so small, I think it was because she was so cooperative, and I think it was because the way she was killed was so close to the fantasy. That was the one that was... it was like it was fantasy," Michael explained. The girls were only fourteen years old when they were murdered.

It was a summer afternoon, around three o'clock on June 13, 1984, when the Roadside Strangler committed the murder that would finally get him caught. He was driving home from work when he passed Wendy Baribeault, who was walking down the side of busy Route 12 in Libson, only a few miles away from his home. Michael Ross pulled the car over and began to speak to this 17-year-old girl; he repeatedly invited her to his company picnic. After a little bit of conversation, Michael forced the beautiful, young girl over a stone wall and into the woods. "When I attacked her, I don't believe that I was in control. I don't think I would've been able to stop," Michael Ross explained his mental state during this attack, "I didn't really feel anything. I knew what was going on and I saw what was going on, but it was more like watching an old film..." Michael then raped the innocent girl and strangled her, just like the others, then entombed her in the stone wall that lined the busy road. The road was so busy, in fact, that there were several eyewitnesses to the attack.

The Investigation of the Roadside Strangler

The police had absolutely no leads on the murderer (a.k.a. The Roadside Strangler) that had taken Connecticut by storm. That was until Wendy Baribeault's body was found. There were dozens of eye witnesses to her attack and composite drawings were created that matched the facial features of local Michael Bruce Ross. Witnesses also noted that the attacker was driving a blue Toyota. Michael Malchik, the investigator assigned to the case, compiled a list of several thousand blue Toyotas. This tiny bit of evidence eventually led investigators directly to Ross' house, which was only three miles away from the location of the crime scene. Michael allegedly dropped hints that he was the murderer upon speaking to the police. "It all had to end," Michael Ross explained. It wasn't long before Michael was called into an interview with police in 1984. After a few hours of grueling interrogation, Michael Bruce Ross confessed to all crimes that he'd committed in Connecticut, but left out the murders in New York. "It's a mystery to me to this day, but it's typical of him," stated Detective Malchik, "Here he is, confessing to six murders, and he thought enough ahead not to tell us about the New York ones. Looking back at it, it's obvious he was thinking of something. He was always thinking two steps ahead. He's got his own agenda, but I couldn't for the life of me tell you what it is."

When Michael confessed to the murders, he seemed very sorrowful and remorseful, but he claimed not to feel a blink of remorse, "I don't want to say that I don't have any remorse, it's just like they weren't real..." Michael explains his feelings towards hid victims in a later interview, "I can't see them as I was killing them, so when I say I don't have any remorse, that doesn't mean that I don't have any regrets, or wish that didn't happen, or there was something that I could do to bring them back or anything – I don't have any feelings towards them. I feel like I should be tormented by them - by what they look like when I was killing them – or tormented by what was happening immediately before I killed them – but none of that's there. None of that's there at all."

"The only time he said he was sorry, was that he was sorry for getting caught," Michael's arresting officer explained, "He (Michael Ross) told me matter-of-factly, he said, 'If you hadn't caught me, I would've just kept on killing, again.'" This eerie statement by itself was enough to put the Roadside Strangler to death immediately, but his strange nature kept investigators questioning his motives behind being so upfront and honest about his heinous crimes. Did he secretly want to get caught? Was this all part of some big plot to instill his insanity?

Anne Cournoyer, Michael's correction counselor, described his mannerisms as he spoke of the horrible crimes that he committed, "One minute he's very, you know, looks like he on the verge of crying, and the next minute he's sort of giggling nervously - or sadistically – you just really don't know. You think that maybe, it's out of nervousness, but he could be getting pleasure out of talking about it."

A full-scale investigation of Michael Bruce Ross' life led to the realization of his wavering mental stability. Michael Ross explained that he could never recall the faces of his victims, even directly after the murders, "You'd think that if you killed someone, you would have the face imprinted in your mind and that you wouldn't be able to get it out of your mind – I don't have that. I never had that," He explained, "The only faces I could see was what was in the newspapers a few days later when they were missing. You know, the high school pictures and 'anybody know where this girl is?' type of thing. When I think of them, that's the picture that I see. I don't see them as they were when I killed them. If you had stopped me right after and gave me a composite drawing of like twelve pictures - you know - some blondes, brunettes, whatever – I wouldn't have been able to pick them out. Even immediately after I killed them."

The names of all eight women were: Dzung Ngoc Tu (25), Paula Perrera (16), Tammy Williams (17), Debra Smith Taylor (23), Robin

Stavinksy (19), April Brunias (14), Leslie Shelley (14), and Wendy Baribeault (17). He was only charged with the murders of the four Connecticut women because the murders of Dzung Ngoc Tu and Paula Perrera took place in New York. He was sentenced to death on July 6, 1987, but remained on death row for eighteen years after his sanity was called into question.

The Curious Case of Michael Bruce Ross

Michael spent the next eighteen years of his life caught in a battle of the Connecticut justice system. In court, a team of psychiatrists flocked to the defense of Mr. Michael Ross. After a parade of psychiatric evaluation, Michael was deemed mentally unwell, due to his dark childhood and his undeniable compulsions. Dr. Fred Berlin, the well-known co-founder of the Johns Hopkins Sexual Disorder Clinic, testified that Ross was struggling with a mental disorder called sexual sadism. Meaning that he gained sexual excitement from the pain and suffering of others. This discovery alone was not enough to save Ross' life, but Michael's claim to lose all self-control during the murders was enough to set back his execution date. Connecticut's state psychiatrist reluctantly agreed that Ross was not mentally capable enough to be responsible for his own actions, and therefore, it was not right to put him to death. Dr. Robert Miller wrote in a private letter, "I can't see how I could testify against psychopathology playing a sufficient role in defendant's behavior." Although this letter was never presented in court, Michael Ross' death sentence was overturned in 1994 and a new sentencing hearing was scheduled in 2000.

Michael Bruce Ross spent most of his time on death row writing about the mental disorder that took hold of his entire life. Michael claimed to have no control over his actions due to his compulsions. He described his sexual sadism as "a mental illness that drove me to rape and kill" and "made me physically unable to control my actions." During his time in prison, Michael still fell victim to his compulsions. It was impossible for him to control his sexual desires, so he spent the first few months of his incarceration reliving the murders. He claimed that he would fantasize these murders over and over again, hurting himself and causing sores from compulsive masturbation. It wasn't very long before he begged for some type of relief from his sexual desires, which came in the form of chemical castration. Ross was given medication that was designed to lower his testosterone levels and it finally relieved him from his sadistic compulsions. Thanks to this medication, Michael Bruce Ross was finally able to think clearly and he was able to see the true nature of his crimes.

The team of prosecutors naturally disagreed with the defense's attempts to lessen his blame. Prosecutors claimed that if he were unable to control his desires, he would've made less calculated attacks. It was reasonable to assume that Ross experienced these sexual desires constantly, which means that he probably experienced these feelings while in public places, or places where his actions could've been seen and reprimanded. Instead, Ross chose his victims very carefully, only acting when the girls were vulnerable and alone. Disproving the defenses' claims more so was the fact that Ross' hid their bodies after the attack, which further strengthened his blame and the case that he knew precisely what he was doing when he was doing it. "I'm not saying I wasn't there or it was multi-personality or any of that type of crap," Michael Ross later explained the strange fog he experienced while he murdered these innocent women, "I was there and I did it, but I wasn't one hundred percent there." To set light upon Mr. Michael Ross' guilt, Prosecutors relied on the "Policeman at the Elbow" test: would Ross have committed the crime even if a policeman had been standing next to him?

The defense team immediately disagreed with the statement that all of Ross' attacks were calculated and well thought out, considering the murder of Ms. Wendy B. who was murdered next to a busy road with several eyewitnesses, "When I attacked her, I don't believe I was in control. I don't think I could've stopped." Michael spoke about the murder that eventually resulted in his incarnation. "Could he control himself? Well, two juries rejected that," Detective Malchik recalls, "As the state's attorney said at the trial if Ross was so out of control, why didn't he just rape the girl in between the yellow lines of Route 12? He made it simple for the juries to understand."

John Blume, a professor at the Law school and co-founder of the Cornell Death Penalty Project, noted the how the jury in Ross' case did not take the opinions of the psychological experts seriously. "The thing that's disturbing," Professor Blume stated, "is that even when the experts all say your client is insane, juries will still reject it." Despite the team of psychologists on Ross' side, claiming that he was completely unable to stop himself from committing these monstrosities, the jury chose not to believe them.

Somewhere in the eighteen years of Michael Ross' incarceration, he decided that he did not deserve to live anymore. Shortly after Michael wrote a story called "It's Time for Me to Die", he reconnected with a woman named Kathy Jaeger, who served as his pastoral advocate that converted Ross to Catholicism. Ross wrote in a newsletter that Jaeger, "was able to breach my defenses and was able to touch my soul as no one else ever has." He later called Ms. Kathy Jaeger "the most important woman in my life" and claimed that "If I were a free man, I would ask her to marry me." Although Kathy rejects his claims to romance, she continued to support Michael Ross throughout his decisions.

After she entered Michael's life, there was a great shift in the nature of his case. Michael was done fighting for his life and the mental condition that wreaked havoc on his entire existence. After his original death sentence was overturned in 1994, the court ordered a new penalty hearing, but instead of going through the hearing with his public defenders, Ross acted as his own attorney. He worked with prosecutor C. Robert Satti to created what was deemed as "death pact" that allowed the imposition of the death penalty without a penalty hearing. "Please allow me to go into the courtroom . . . to accept the death penalty as punishment for my actions," Ross wrote in a letter to Satti. "I'm not asking you to do this for me, but for the families involved, who do not deserve to suffer further and who, in some small way, might gain a sense of peace of mind by these actions and my execution." The "death pact" was rejected by the judge as a "short cut" involving a human life, so Michael Ross flip-flopped back into his old ways. Ross returned to his defense team and reverted back into fighting for his life, claiming that his crimes were merely a product of his mental illness. He was resentenced to death soon after.

Jaeger said that Ross's sudden acceptance of death was a sincere attempt to provide closure for the families of his victims, "He told me, 'You know I don't want to do this. But I have to.' He just really felt anguish over what he had done. Really, really harsh anguish and self-loathing. Contrary to media reports, he doesn't want to die. He wishes that the justice system got it right years ago and gave him life sentences because he does have a mental illness. And the sad thing is, if they had done that, the families of his victims wouldn't have been re-victimized [by the ongoing appeals]. Michael is trying, in essence, to save them from any more of that."

Whether his acceptance of the death sentence was sincere, or not, Michael Bruce Ross was sentenced to death by lethal injection on May 13, 2005. He chose not to speak any last words before his death and died peacefully in the execution chair. Some family members believed that his death was too peaceful. Debbie Dupuis, Robin Stavinsky's sister, stated that she thought she would "feel closure" but instead just "felt anger" as she watched Ross simply lay there, go to sleep and die.

The state of Connecticut finally decided to end the life of the Roadside Strangler and put an end to the anguish that the families had to endure. After a very tragic and dark lifetime, Michael Bruce Ross and his sadistic compulsions were finally laid to rest.

Conclusion

Michael Bruce Ross is the type of cold, calculating, manipulative killer that we only read about in horror novels. His crimes almost seem too heartless and brutal to be true, but the victims of the Roadside Strangler would tell you that he is nothing but a cruel reality. In only a few years, Michael assaulted a countless number of women and murdered eight. Although he was only charged with four murders, Ross was forced to withstand eighteen long years of debate over his life sentence. In prison, he transitioned from a vicious killer who was truly non-remorseful for his brutal crimes to a man who seemed to genuinely regret his life choices and the pain that he subjected. Towards the end of his life, Ross begged for removal from his troubled existence, not only for himself but to end the long and grueling process of the legal system. Despite his transition into humanity, Michael Bruce Ross never took full blame for his actions. He flip-flopped between blaming his childhood, his compulsions, and his interpersonal relationships for these terrible crimes. He claimed to never feel any guilt or remorse for his actions, simply because he wasn't completely there while they were taking place. During these attacks, Michael claims that he was under some type of spell, some type of fog that completely disconnected him from his actions. He was completely able to murder and rape these innocent women without feeling guilt or remorse, or even being able to recall the very faces of his victims', only moments after their attack. Michael Ross was an extremely troubled man who suffered from a very extreme case of sexual sadism. Michael explained his cruel, heartless, attacks with vivid details and an undetached tone of voice. The scariest part about his calm demeanor is the monotone way that he described the way he stole the lives of these young, innocent women. He speaks as if he were not responsible for killing these beautiful and young women, although he willingly confesses to the murders. He claimed that he was merely a victim of his sexual compulsions since his college years and the women he attacked were merely in the wrong place at the wrong time. Whether his desires were really uncontrollable or if it was merely an excuse, Michael Bruce Ross' case remains to be one of the most perplexing cases in American history. His mere mental condition was enough to perplex the entire state of Connecticut – how could this well-spoken, articulate man with such a great personality, commit these terrible crimes? Why didn't anyone notice his decline and stop it? What was it that made this seemingly normal man snap into the Roadside Strangler? Although the answers to these questions are uncertain, they definitely are unnerving. Michael Ross was created by circumstances, by his dark upbringing, and a lifetime of people letting him slip through the cracks. Everyone saw him as an average, everyday college student, so no one thought to ask. The woman that he murdered were sadly only stepping stones into the downward spiral into his sickness and they were eventually caused the end of his vicious, murderous cycle.

STOCKWELL STRANGLER: The True Story of Kenneth Erskine

NATALIE MARSHALL

Kenneth Erskine, known as "The Stockwell Strangler" due to the geographic proximities of his murders, was a deeply troubled young man who had demonstrated worrisome signs of violence and schizophrenia from a young age. He was a gerontophile in that he had an unnatural sexual attraction to the elderly. Gerontophilia, essentially, is the opposite of pedophilia. Erskine would break into elderly men's and women's London flats and strangle them while they were in bed; after which he would rape and/or sodomize most of them. To demonstrate his own warped sense of love for his victims he would cross their arms across their chest, close their eyes, and tuck them into bed. Also, perhaps to hide his shame, he would turn his victims' family photographs face down. There was much speculation among mental health professionals that Erskine also suffered from schizophrenia from a very young age.

He was eventually convicted of seven murders and one attempted murder and sentenced to life in prison in 1988 at the age of 25. However, in July 2009, following an appeal his murder convictions were reduced to manslaughter on the grounds of diminished capacity and he received a hospital order to serve his life sentences at Broadmoor Hospital. While he has the potential to be granted parole in 2028, the trial judge's original order was that Erskine should spend at least 40 years behind bars, thus making him at least 65 years of age before potential eligibility for release.

Early Life

Kenneth Erskine was born in Hammersmith, London in July 1963. His mother Margaret was British and his father Charles was from Antigua. He was one of four boys, had an average IQ when tested at eight years old, and was remembered by neighbors to be a "chubby, Bible reading soul"; however, he became increasingly violent and difficult to control. For example, as a child, Erskine had tried to hang his younger brother, John, twice.

Erskine was then sent to a series of schools for maladjusted and troubled children where he received his formal education. He frequently and violently attacked his teachers and classmates and was identified as inhabiting a fantasy world with murderous impulses. In his own private fantasy world he would take on the role of Lawrence of Arabia, attacking and tying up smaller and weaker children—a theme that would resurface when he targeted the weaker elderly during his murder spree. During a school-sponsored swimming outing he had attempted to drown several classmates by holding their heads under the water until teachers were forced to intervene. He set fires at school and once pushed a classmate off of a moving bus. On another occasion he stabbed a teacher in the hand with a pair of scissors. In another event, a psychiatric nurse who tried to examine Erskine was taken hostage by him as he held a pair of scissors to her throat. He strangled the classroom guinea pig. Whenever any female staff tried to be empathetic and show him any type of affection he would expose his genitals or rub up against them.

There was frequent talk that Erskine demonstrated clear signs and symptoms of schizophrenia as a teenager but nothing ever came out of it. He never had therapy or medication or any real psychiatric evaluation.

By the time Erskine was 16 years of age he had turned to drugs and particularly enjoyed inhalants. This latest display of misbehavior was too much for his mother who eventually kicked him out of the house, forcing him to survive on his own. When Erskine tried to give his younger brother marijuana she finally disowned him. He never saw any of his family members ever again and was forced to spend the next seven years of his life "drifting through the twilight world of London's homeless and rootless" living in squats and hostels in Brixton and Stockwell and getting involved with petty crime which primarily took the shape of failed burglaries on primarily the elderly.

Erskine's violent tendencies continued to worsen.

When he was 18 he stabbed a young male with whom he was having a homosexual relationship at the time. Erskine had burst into his boyfriend's bedroom and stabbed and slashed at his body while he lay in bed. Whereas this may have been the first attack of someone in bed it was a glaring omen of the terror he would wreak in six years.

Erskine was described my many who knew him as a persistent loner who drifted through life and due to no direction of any type of social support system started a life of crime. Erskine was also a Rastafarian due to his Caribbean heritage but was shunned by fellow Rastafarians due to his habit of theft.

An unsuccessful burglar, he was jailed on many occasions.

Among Erskine's favorite "drugs" were solvents—such as glue—which he would inhale. Among the most oft-cited short term effects of huffing glue are hallucinations, delusions, and hostility. Long-term effects include depression, irritability, memory impairment, diminished intelligence, and serious and sometimes irreversible brain damage. There continues to be speculation as to whether Erskine was born with his psychopathic tendencies (nature) or whether his upbringing and environmental stimuli were to blame for his problems (nurture). The consensus is that a combination of factors worked together to create Erskine's sick and murderous persona.

Erskine subsequently spent considerable time in Borstals—youth detention centers—due to being apprehended following his many failed burglaries. While in one for burglary in 1982 Erskine would paint and draw pictures of elderly people in bed with gags in their mouths, with daggers in them, or burned to death. Additional pieces of "artwork" included headless figures with blood spurting out from their necks, people holding human hearts in their hands, disemboweled people, screaming faces, and copious pools of blood. Again, this was a chilling omen of what was to come. In one documentary about Kenneth Erskine and his crimes, one of his cellmates at Borstal, named James, described how horrific Erskine's paintings were and how he would frequently smile and laugh while painting them. As Erskine's only "friend" James became his confidant as well. The two would play chess to pass the time and then there were Erskine's disturbing paintings. James stated in an interview that Erskine always spoke very quietly—rarely above a whisper—and was very weird.

Borstal doctors were concerned enough to the point of asking the authorities not to ever free Erskine because they were seriously worried that he might try to replicate his paintings; however, he was, in fact, released and four years later he would begin his killing spree.

The Crimes

At some point Erskine decided to act out his fantasies and began to murder. He is classified as a geographically-stable serial killer who confined his murders to a specific area. As Erskine had no vehicle and roamed around the Stockwell area frequently confining his murders to this area was likely due to simple necessity.

The Stockwell section of South London is a favored place for the elderly to retire. In the summer of 1986, however, a serial killer conducted a reign of terror throughout the community that resulted in seven known deaths—and possibly another four—attributable to The Stockwell Strangler.

Eileen Nancy Emms, 78

Emms was a 78-year-old retired schoolteacher who lived in an "unkempt basement flat" on West Hill Road in Wandsworth. She was sexually assaulted and strangled by Erskine on 6 April 1986.

Emms' body was found on 9 April 1987 by her home help who, upon knocking on her bedroom door and receiving no response one morning, let herself in to find Emms in bed with the covers pulled up to her chin, seemingly asleep. There were no obvious marks upon her body. Initially, the cause of death was attributed to natural causes. The doctor called to the scene estimated that she died approximately three days earlier and signed a death certificate that stated natural causes.

Once the victim's home help noticed that her small portable television was missing, the police were called.

During her autopsy, the medical examiner revealed that Emms had been strangled by bare hands. There was heavy bruising to her chest which strongly suggested that her assailant had kneeled atop her while strangling her. Further examination revealed that she had been sodomized as the assailant had left semen around her anus.

A short Afro-Caribbean head hair was found on her sheet.

Janet Crockett, 67

Janet Crockett was Erskine's first July 1987 victim. She was chairwoman of her local tenant's association. Her body was found on 9 June in her flat in the Overton Estate in Stockwell. She had been strangled but, unlike Erskine's first victim—and subsequent ones—she was not sexually assaulted.

Police were able to immediately conclude that she had been murdered as she had considerable bruising on her chest due to sustaining two broken ribs as a result of someone kneeling on her while she was strangled to death. Additionally, her nightgown had been ripped from her body and folded neatly and placed upon a bedside chair.

Police also noticed that framed family photographs on the bedroom mantel had been placed face down or turned around. This action would be repeated at several of his crime scenes and speculation abounds as to what Erskine's underlying motive for doing this was. Some psychological experts have surmised that his anger at his own parents' rejection without a healthy outlet for his emotions led to an insane jealousy of normal family ties. Another hypothesis was that he felt ashamed at his actions and didn't want any "witnesses."

Police were able to find a smudged thumbprint on a displaced planter and a palm print on the bathroom window.

Pathologist Dr. Iain West conducted Crockett's autopsy and compared it to Emms. He concluded that their methods of strangulation were similar. He stated that with weaker elderly victims unconsciousness would occur within 30 second and death after approximately three minutes. While Crockett's and Emms' murders were similar—and that they were both elderly—police had nothing else to link the two victims.

Frederick Prentice, 73

In the early hours of 27 June, 73-year-old retired engineer Frederick Prentice was asleep in his council-run elderly people's home on Cedars Road in Clapham when he was awakened by the sounds of someone entering his bedroom. He saw a young man enter and Prentice turned on his bedside lamp and ordered the intruder to leave. Erskine then pounced atop the old man, placed his index finger to his own mouth as a threat for Prentice to be quiet, and then sat upon his chest where he alternated squeezing his windpipe powerfully, then relaxing his grip, and repeated this multiple times. Prentice told police that his assailant had whispered only one word over and over: "Kill." Prentice was able to push the alarm button near his bed which caused his assailant to leave.

After talking to Prentice the police were fairly confident that all of the victims thus far were, in fact, linked. A shoeprint found at the scene would also serve to connect this attack with some of the other murders.

Prentice would later identify Erskine in a lineup.

Valentine Gleim, 84, and Zbigniew Stabrawa, 94

The next day Erskine murdered 84-year-old World War II veteran Valentine Gleim and 94-year-old Polish immigrant Zbigniew Stabrawa in their adjoining rooms at Somerville Hastings House, an old folks' home on Stockwell Park Crescent. Both men had been manually strangled and sodomized.

The intruder had been seen by alert night duty staff but had vanished before the police arrived. Point of entry was, again, determined to be an open window. Staff were also able to see Erskine fleeing the scene and estimated his height at approximately five-feet-eight-inches with a slim frame so at least now investigators had a clue about their suspect.

Of particular concern in these two cases was the discovery of a used flannel towel and electric shaver which suggested that the murderer had calmly washed up and shaved after killing two people.

Approximately one hour prior to the double homicide an elderly woman in a Stockwell old folks' home was attacked while she was in bed by a man grabbing her arm. She fought off her assailant so vehemently that he had to run off. Her description of Erskine matched Prentice's.

William Carmen, 82

Two weeks after his previous double homicide, Erskine struck again by strangling and sexually assaulting 82-year-old widower William Carmen on 8 July. This time he threw a monkey wrench at detectives by murdering on the other side of the Thames river, in Islington, North London. Carmen was discovered dead in his bed in his flat on the Marques Estate by his daughter. As was the case with Erskine's other victims, Carmen was in bed with the covers pulled up neatly to his chin and had been sodomized.

This time there was clear evidence of ransacking and theft as approximately £400 of Carmen's savings was missing. Family photos were also placed face down or turned around.

William Downes, 74

On 20 July the body of 74-year-old William Downes was found by his son in his Holles House on Overton Road flat in Brixton; the same location where Erskine's second victim, Crockett, lived. He was naked and in bed with the covers pulled up to his chin, his eyes closed, and his arms folded across his chest—classic Erskine signature. Downes' son had reminded him to keep his windows locked firmly at night a few days ago so as not to fall victim to the Strangler but he failed to heed these instructions and point of entry was, again, determined to be through an unlocked window.

Downes had been strangled and sexually assaulted like the majority of Erskine's other victims. There were semen stains on the sheets.

Investigators lifted a palm print from the kitchen wall and another from the garden gate which were eventually matched to the prints found at Crockett's home. Finding the owner of these prints, however, was not as easy as the process is today. In 1986, while fingerprints were on file on computer discs at Scotland Yard, palm prints were not. Investigators had a stack of four million files; however, by concentrating on London-based burglars and petty thieves, they were able to compile a more workable load. They were subsequently able to match the prints to those Erskine, a small-time crook with an extensive rap sheet for burglary.

Unfortunately, the police did not know where to find Erskine and while they were looking he struck again, killing his final victim.

Florence Tisdall, 80

80-year-old partially blind and deaf Florence Tisdall was found in her apartment at Ranelagh Gardens near Putney Bridge on 24 July. The caretaker of the apartments noticed her walker in the communal corridor and knew something was wrong as Tisdall was unable to get around without it. He found her strangled, sexually assaulted, and with broken ribs as a result of her killer sitting atop her chest. She had spent the previous day watching the televised wedding of the Duke and Duchess of York—Prince Andrew and Sarah Ferguson—even having her own hair done especially for the big event. Tisdall had lived in an almost empty block of flats where she had resided for the past 60 years. A cat lady, she had left her windows open so the cats could come and go as they pleased and this is how Erskine got into her flat.

It was at this scene where Erskine made, perhaps, his biggest mistake. Detectives knew immediately that Tisdall had been murdered because she was found in her nightgown, tucked into bed with the covers up by her chin. In reality, however, Tisdall's neighbors who frequently checked on her because of her disabilities stated that she always slept atop the covers in the clothing she had been wearing that day. When Erskine undressed Tisdall to rape her, he attempted to cover up his misdeeds by making it look as though she went to bed as usual and died of natural causes. Family photos were also placed face down or turned around as was the case at the Crockett crime scene.

One of Tisdall's neighbors stated that she saw Erskine near the victim's flat shortly after the murder had occurred "looking disgusted with himself." Thinking this to be odd she promptly notified the police.

All of Erskine's victims were pensioners and in all but one case there was evidence of sexual assault that took the form of sodomy; however, investigators and forensic specialists cannot say whether it occurred before or after the victims' death.

Investigation and Arrest

After the Crockett murder, Scotland Yard's Serious Crimes Squad Detective Chief Superintendent Ken Thompson—a Scotsman with 26 years' experience—was put in charge of the case and given over 200 detectives to devote to the search for The Stockwell Strangler. Interestingly, Erskine was originally nicknamed "The Heatwave Killer" because the murders occurred during the summer; however, when the majority of his murders occurred in and around Stockwell this nickname was changed. Further, plainclothes officers would stand guard throughout the night wherever the elderly lived.

At the height of the investigation, as many as 350 law enforcement officers were on the Strangler case which included 150 detectives and senior officers from the C1 Murder Squad who worked out of five separate incident rooms throughout London which were linked to a special Home Office computer. This network was called HOLMUS and was used to prevent wasting time by cross checking paperwork which proved to be detrimental to the investigation for Peter Sutcliff, The Yorkshire Ripper. Other police officers set up fixed observation points in neighborhoods with a high population of elderly residents and instituted extra patrols.

A psychologist was enlisted to create a profile of the Strangler and to provide potential insight into his signature to determine whether he was attempting to cover his tracks or was fulfilling some bizarre fantasy. The suspect was determined to be suffering from gerontophilia; or a sexual attraction to the elderly and the complete opposite of its better known opposite, pedophilia. Speculation abounded as to whether the killer's sexual paraphilia was a result of some relationship problems with his grandparents. Additionally, as his victims were all selected at random, authorities could not link the victims together with the hopes of finding some commonality between them that would enable them to identify and apprehend the man responsible.

The suspect was classified as a process-focused serial killer. The majority of serial killers are of this type; the other being act-focused wherein their own psychological gratification from the kill itself is the underlying cause. Instead, process-focused killers achieve a hedonistic psychological "reward." These types frequently "get off" on the method of their kill and they enjoy the perverse sexual thrill that accompanies the act of killing. The literature identifies four types of process-focused serial killers: gain in which the killer kills for profit or personal gain; thrill in which the act of killing gives the killer a rush or a high; power in which the killer enjoys dominating and manipulating victims and while sex is usually involved it is primarily tertiary to the kill itself; and lust wherein murder is associated with sexual pleasure and this type of killer will commonly have sex while in the process or killing or may engage in necrophilia after death. As far as Erskine is concerned, he can be classified in multiple subtypes. First, since he did rob his victims and steal money he demonstrates some elements of the gain process-focused serial killer. Secondly, he did obtain a rush or high from killing his victims and, therefore, does demonstrate some elements of a thrill killer. This element is particularly salient when he was seen by a witness—who would later testify against him—getting sick on the sidewalk after his final kill near where his last victim was found. The act of his getting sick appears to be directly attributed to the thrill her received from killing and having sex with his victim. Finally, since Erskine likely sodomized his victims after he killed them his sexual fantasies were of a higher priority than is typically the case for power killers. Thus, he demonstrates elements more aligned with a lust killer.

Coupled with the fact that Erskine targeted the same type of people and that he engaged in specific rituals which were part of his signature makes Erskine a classic serial killer. His smaller size likely contributed to his choice of the elderly as his victims because in their weakened conditions he wouldn't have much trouble overpowering them.

The palm prints were the most damning evidence investigators had at that point; however, they only placed Erskine at two of the murder scenes. Despite similarities among all of the victims' crime scenes, the fact that Erskine wasn't cooperating with police required detectives to find other evidence. Investigators from Scotland Yard took the unusual step of distributing his Erskine's picture to the media to try to find more witnesses and potential leads by hopefully jog people's memories as to whether anyone may remember seeing him. Thompson also did something very uncommon; he appeared on television, appealing to Erskine to turn himself in.

After Tisdall's death the search for Erskine intensified even more than was already the case; however, being that he was a drifter with no permanent address or any real belongings to speak of they had to search through the hundreds of hostels and squats in South London. His life was so devoid of meaning and friends to help detectives find him.

Investigators got their big break when they realized that since the suspect was likely unemployed that he would be receiving social security and unemployment benefits. Upon further investigation they discovered that Erskine picked up his benefits on alternating Mondays from a Department of Health and Social Security office in Southwark, South London, and that he was due to collect his next check on 28 July. The building was placed under surveillance and when Erskine turned up, right on time, he was arrested and handcuffed without any struggle.

Whereas items and cash from the victims' homes were, in fact, missing, police did not believe that robbery was the driving motive in the homicides. There were neither signs of struggle nor any signs of forced entry. Police surmised that Erskine entered the flats through unsecured windows.

Forensic evidence linking the cases relied upon the fact that the victims were all murdered in similar ways: by the assailant kneeling on the victims' chests and then placing his left hand over their mouths and strangling them with his right hand. The semen collected at nearly all crime scenes suggested the same genetic fingerprint in that the same suspect was responsible for all of the sexual assaults. Additionally, there was a single hair found in Emms' flat, as well as matching shoeprints from three of the scenes.

A hairdresser informed investigators that Erskine had approached her wanting his head and pubic hair bleached. While she agreed to the former she refused the latter. Apparently, while he was sitting in the shop waiting for the bleach to take effect he self-applied the bleach to his pubic region and eyebrows, the latter resulting in his getting chemicals in his eyes and requiring assistance in washing it out.

When questioned by Detective Inspector Brian Jackson and other detectives, Erskine's responses indicated that the detectives' jobs were to be much more difficult than they thought. Erskine spent the majority of the interrogation giggling, staring out of the window or into the sky, or masturbating. After he was arrested, psychologists placed Erskine's mental age at 11 even though he was 24 at the time. He had first denied that he was, indeed, The Stockwell Strangler claiming instead to be a petty burglar who had no motive to kill anyone. After vehemently denying his culpability and blameworthiness in the string of murders and seeing that he wasn't getting anywhere, Erskine then changed his tune and said, "I don't remember killing anyone. I could have done it without knowing it. I am not sure if I did it." He also tried to blame the murders on a whispering female voice in his head. He once stated, "It tries to think for me. It says it will kill me if it gets me," and, "It blanks things from my mind."

He was clearly disturbed but not a fool in any sense. In fact, when searched, detectives found ten bank and building society accounts that Erskine had opened to hide the proceeds of his crimes. During the three-month span of murders, he had deposited over £3,000; quite a large sum of money for someone who was unemployed. This included a £350 deposit into one of his accounts on the morning after the Carmen murder. It was evident at this point that Erskine was amassing profits from his burglaries while simultaneously collecting unemployment benefits. This demonstrated that whereas Erskine did suffer from some degree of mental retardation and likely some psychosexual paraphilia he was not stupid by any means. In fact, he told detectives that his motive was to achieve notoriety. He said, "I wanted to be famous ... I thought I would never get caught."

During a lineup—or identity parade as it is called in England—surviving victim Frederick Prentice was able to definitively identify Erskine. Another woman who had witnessed Erskine vomiting on the sidewalk near Putney Bridge a mere 200 yards from the scene of the final murder on the night in question also picked Erskine out of a lineup.

Trial and Conviction

Erskine's trial commenced at the Old Bailey on 12 January 1988. He pled not guilty to the charges of seven murders and the attempted murder of Prentice. During his trial he would stare out the window or down at his feet as was the case when he was interrogated. When details of the murders were brought up, Erskine would masturbate.

The jury heard him confess to the burglaries of the deceased victims; however, he claimed that someone else must have followed him and killed the individuals after he had left. Nobody was buying this story.

After an 18-day trial, the jury unanimously found him guilty on all eight counts and he was sentenced to seven life terms plus 12 years for attempted murder with a recommended minimum of 40 years; one of the heaviest penalties ever handed out in British legal history. However, diagnosis of schizophrenia and other mental illnesses pursuant to the Mental Health Act of 1983 led to a successful appeal of Erskine's murder charges which were eventually reduced to manslaughter. He is currently serving his time at the Broadmoor Hospital.

In addition to his seven known victims, the police suspected Erskine of four other murders for which he has never been charged due to insufficient evidence to prove that he was, in fact, the murderer.

John Jordan, 57

On 4 February 1986, 57-year-old John Jordan was found in his Josephine Avenue flat in Brixton strangled beside his bed.

Charles Quarrell, 73

73-year-old Charles Quarrell was found suffocated in his bed on King James Street in Suffolk on 6 May. He had two handkerchiefs stuffed into the back of his throat, effectively blocking his windpipe.

Wilfred Parkes, 70

70-year-old Wilfred Parkes was found on 28 May in his Stockwell flat, suffocated and in bed. A nearby pillow was presumed to have been the murder weapon.

Trevor Thomas, 75

On 12 July 75-year-old Trevor Thomas was found dead in the bath at his home on Barton Court, Clapham. As Thomas had been dead for quite a while there was inadequate forensic evidence for investigators to link his murder to the others; thus resulting in Erskine not being charged with his death even though Thomas was almost certainly one of his victims.

As mentioned, Erskine has never been charged with these additional deaths; however, police were so confident that Erskine murdered them that they effectively closed the book on all of these cases. There is also much speculation that he likely killed prior to his first known victim—such as was the case with Mr. Jordan—and that because of his choice of victims their deaths may have simply been attributed to natural causes.

Aftermath

There is not much more information on Erskine due to a lack of any detailed studies of him as is commonly the case with other serial killers where the literature is rife with speculation as to what influences led to the individual turning to serial murder. His only possessions were meager clothes and some books from the building society. Other than a post-arrest diagnosis of schizophrenia, the mind of Kenneth Erskine remains mostly shrouded in mystery. In fact, his mentally-disturbed state has worsened to the point where he has been told that he will never be released from Broadmoor Hospital.

Psychiatrists have never been able to fully penetrate his mind and discover what makes him tick. He clearly has a problem differentiating fantasy from reality and appears to be locked in his own childlike world. However, there is one incident that clearly demonstrates his understanding between right and wrong. On 23 February 1996, Erskine prevented the possible murder of Peter Sutcliffe, known as the "Yorkshire Ripper" by alerting guards while another inmate, Paul Wilson, attempted to strangle Sutcliffe with the flexible cord from a pair of stereo headphones. Erskine was able to restrain Wilson from inflicting further injury upon Sutcliffe until guards arrived.

Erskine found himself on the receiving end of an assault. On Christmas Eve in 1997 he was attacked by fellow inmate, 34-year-old

Keith Hanger. Hanger was serving time for the 1992 shooting of his friend after having escaped from prison. He walked up to Erskine and squirted liquid from an aerosol can into his face before lighting it with a lighter. Erskine was taken to Frimley Park Hospital in Surrey, in agonizing pain and worried that he would lose his eyesight; however, his temporary blindness was just that—temporary.

Psychiatrists continue to attempt to probe Erskine's mind trying to uncover more and more of his psyche toward, perhaps, finding what makes him tick. Currently, he is unable to answer for his crimes, as demonstrated by the reduced sentence due to diminished capacity.titutes during the interrogation, which would explain why his DNA was found on three of the young girls' bodies. He focused on Tania Nichols, telling a story about how he picked her up with the intention to have sexual relations, but changed his mind and returned her back to the red light district. Again, this account differed from the one that he originally gave to investigators. On February 21, 2008, Steve Wright was charged as guilty on all five counts of murder after eight hours of deliberation. He received a life sentence without any chance of parole. On February 22, 2008, Wright was taken to prison, where he'll be forced to live out the rest of his years behind bars.

Wright is still alive to this day and he is having a terrible time in prison. His twisted state of mind after imprisonment is outlined in his letter to his father: "...I just wish everyone would get along and work towards a family unit because all the bickering and point scoring against each other is really getting me down it seems you are pulling me one way and pam is pulling me the other and in the end, something will give and it just seems to me that person will be me and that is the last thing that I want at the moment has I am sure you do as well because if I start to fall apart at the seams I don't think I could cope in here I need to be strong to cope with this nightmare like that but you said in the paper that when you looked [in] my eyes you would know whether I was guilty or not that really hurt me it was like a knife in the heart for you to even contemplate that I could even be capable of such a terrible crime. You say you want to help me the only way that will happen is if you make the effort to work together because all this he said she said you must understand is not doing my frame of mind any good I just want it to stop I do love you dad..."